W9-AQT-677

George Peele

Twayne's English Authors Series

Arthur F. Kinney, Editor

University of Massachusetts, Amherst

TEAS 356

[illegible]
[illegible]
[illegible]
[illegible]
Brauely ran Beaforde & his staues he brake
right happely for his highe ladys sake.
Compton of Compton came in shininge armes
well mounted & appointed for ye feilde.
A gallant Lorde: richely arayde was hee
he & his trayne: Clio recoute his fame
recorde wth me his loue to Learninges Lore
& valeante demeanors on this hollydaye
Shorte will I bee in processe of his praise:
Coragiously he ran & wth the best
from forthe the feilde bare honor & his crest
Carew was well acquainted wth the place
& to the tilt prowdely he made approache
his steede well taught himselfe fitted in all
fell to

Anglorum Feriae, lines 237–54 in George Peele's handwriting.
(British Library Additional Manuscript 21432, f. 9r).
Reproduced courtesy of The British Library.

George Peele

By A. R. Braunmuller

Twayne Publishers • Boston

For L. B. B.

George Peele

A. R. Braunmuller

Published by Twayne Publishers
A Division of G. K. Hall & Company
70 Lincoln Street
Boston, Massachusetts 02111

Book Production by Marne B. Sultz

Book Design by Barbara Anderson

Printed on permanent/durable acid-free
paper and bound in the United States of
America.

Library of Congress Cataloging in Publication Data.

Braunmuller, A. R., 1945–
George Peele.

(Twayne's English authors series ; TEAS 356)
Bibliography: p. 151
Includes index.
1. Peele, George, 1558?–1597?—Criticism and
interpretation. I. Title. II. Series.
PR2737.B7 1983 822′.3 83–199
ISBN 0–8057–6842–4

Contents

About the Author

A. R. Braunmuller received his early education in Europe and the United States, the B.A. from Stanford University (1967), and the Ph.D. in English Literature from Yale University (1971). Since 1971, he has taught Renaissance and modern drama at the University of California, Los Angeles, where he is Professor of English. He has edited Bertolt Brecht's two adaptations of John Webster's *The Duchess of Malfi* (New York: Random House, 1974; London: Eyre Methuen, 1976) and the Auden-Kallman translation of Brecht's *The Rise and Fall of the City of Mahagonny* (Boston: Godine, 1976). Scholarly journals have published his essays on such playwrights as Robert Greene, George Chapman, Henrik Ibsen, and Harold Pinter; he has also published articles on bibliographical topics (Elizabethan printing and manuscript letter-books). In 1983, the University of Delaware Press will publish his edition of a Renaissance manuscript containing letters by the dramatists George Chapman and Ben Jonson, and in 1982 the Malone Society published his edition of *The Captive Lady,* an early seventeenth-century play. Professor Braunmuller won the Harvey L. Eby Memorial Award for the Art of Teaching at UCLA in 1980.

Editor's Note

A. R. Braunmuller's fine study of the most neglected of the University Wits, who with Greene and Marlowe helped to pioneer the greatest age of English drama, argues that the work of George Peele was shaped by his unique and searching imagination, his insistence on the political relevance of pageantry and drama, his keen sense of diverse audiences, and his sometimes wayward but always fascinating and instructive craftsmanship. In *The Araygnement of Paris* Peele tries singlehandedly to transform the progress pageant into sophisticated court drama; some puzzles of the apparently intractable *Old Wives Tale* yield resolution when we see how thoroughly Peele has rethought and reworked folk motifs; *David and Bethsabe,* the best of the latter-day biblical plays in Renaissance England, experiments with the dramatic crosspatterning of vertical and horizontal relationships; *The Battle of Alcazar* and *Edward I* rearrange history to parallel contemporary events and to reveal the profound political anxiety of Peele's day. In all of this, we witness Peele's surprising variety and range. Although Peele's associates measured his work with undiluted praise, we have neglected him because much of his meaning has seemed lost in the recesses of our literary past. It is Braunmuller's achievement to rediscover Peele's significance by recovering the poet in his time. This study of George Peele bids fair to become a standard work for some time to come.

Arthur F. Kinney

Preface and Acknowledgments

This study begins with the assumption that we cannot fully understand an artist's work unless we understand that artist's social situation and how his or her society values art. Whether or not this assumption is generally true, it seems to apply to a popular writer, like George Peele, in a culture which was exceedingly ambivalent about the purpose and nature of art, like the England of Elizabeth I. Throughout this book, therefore, I consider the links among political, economic, and social facts and Peele's diverse literary production. This enterprise does not mean, however, that we can or should ignore the artist's individual contribution, or the influence of literary tradition and literary contemporaries, or indeed the more diffuse pressure of popular sentiment and prejudice. Fellow writers and the heterogeneous Elizabethan audience demonstrably affected Peele's writings, and again, I have tried to show how this influence may have operated.

Peele's most memorable writing aims at theatrical performance (the court theater, the public theater, civic celebrations) or records quasi-theatrical events (Accession Day festivities and other courtly occasions). This fact alone requires us to consider his audience(s) and to examine his abilities as a theater-craftsman. Consequently, my literary and dramatic analysis emphasizes the occasions and the possible enactments of the writing. Neither Peele's good dramatic sense nor the larger issue of his place in Renaissance society has received full scrutiny. The former has been generally dismissed and the latter ignored. Other critics have established Peele's lyric and verbal brilliance, and I have therefore commented on only a few instances of his distinguished achievements as a stylist.

In quoting early printed texts, I have sometimes changed capitalization and modernized *i/j, u/v,* and the "long" *ſ*. All citations of Peele's work refer to *The Life and Works of George Peele,* gen. ed., Charles Tyler Prouty, 3 vols. (New Haven: Yale University Press, 1952–1970).

Most of the research for this book was conducted at the Huntington Library and the British Library; I thank their staffs, especially David Paisey, formerly superintendant of the North Library. The Academic Senate Research Committee of the University of California, Los Angeles, generously assisted my work. C. T. Corman, Jeffrey Aaron, Peter Merrill and Susan Stanton helped check the manuscript, and Jeanette Gilkison typed much of it.

I should like to add a few more private acknowledgments, not to share responsibility, but to give thanks. Richard Proudfoot gave generously of his well-considered opinions and freely of his large knowledge, including the rare experience of having directed *The Old Wives Tale.* Lauro Martines discussed and improved many of the ideas in this book; I hope he will spare a thought for Peele as he writes about Elizabethan literature. Robert Dent, A. S. G. Edwards, and Louis Montrose helped me in many ways.

The dedicatee has read most, and approved some, of this book.

A. R. Braunmuller

University of California, Los Angeles

Chronology

1556	George Peele born in London, shortly before 25 July.
1562	James Peele, the playwright's father, appointed Clerk of Christ's Hospital, London, shortly before 10 November; George Peele entered reading and writing school of Christ's Hospital.
1565	Entered grammar school of Christ's Hospital.
1571	Matriculated at Broadgates Hall, Oxford, about April.
1574	Became a student at Christ Church, Oxford, by December.
?1574–1577	Translated a play on Iphigenia (by Euripides?) now lost.
1577	Graduated B.A., Oxford.
1579	Graduated M.A., Oxford.
1580	Married Ann Christian, daughter of an Oxford merchant.
1580–1581	Lived in Oxford; wrote(?) *A Tale of Troy.*
1581	Moved to London; may have written Lord Mayor's pageant.
?1581–1584	Wrote *The Araygnement of Paris* for court performance.
1582	Wrote prefatory poem for Thomas Watson's *Hekatompathia,* before 31 March.
1583	Assisted in presenting two plays at Christ Church, Oxford, in June.
1584	*The Araygnement of Paris* published; Peele may have written a mayoral pageant.
1585	Wrote mayoral pageant, performed in October and published. James Peele died in London, 30 December.
1586	George Peele may have written mayoral pageant.

?1587 Ann Christian Peele may have died.

1587 Peele may have written mayoral pageant.

1588 Wrote mayoral pageant (not extant).

?1589 Wrote *The Battle of Alcazar.*

1589 Wrote (before 23 February) and published *A Farewell . . . to . . . Norris and . . . Drake;* published *A Tale of Troy.* Wrote (before 1 August) and published *An Eclogue Gratulatory.*

1590 Wrote and published *Polyhymnia* late in the year.

?1590–1594 Wrote *The Old Wives Tale.*

?1591 Peele may have married Mary Yates.

1591 *The Hunting of Cupid* (extant in fragments) entered for publication, 26 July; wrote *Descensus Astraeae,* performed before 29 October, and published.

?1592–1594 Wrote *David and Bethsabe.*

1593 Wrote (before 23 June) and published *The Honour of the Garter. The Praise of Chastity* published in *The Phoenix Nest. Edward I* published.

1594 *The Battle of Alcazar* published; *David and Bethsabe* entered for printing.

1595 Wrote *Anglorum Feriae; The Old Wives Tale* published.

1596 Died in London, 9 November.

1599 *David and Bethsabe* published; *Edward I* reprinted.

1600 Excerpts printed in *England's Helicon* and *England's Parnassus.*

1604 *The Tale of Troy* (revised version of *A Tale of Troy*) published.

Chapter One

The Poor Fellows That Live by It: Writing for a Living in Elizabethan England

The Bodleian Library, Oxford, holds the unique and tattered copy of a brief script George Peele wrote for the 1585 pageant celebrating the installation of Wolstan Dixi as Lord Mayor of London. At the very end appears the phrase: "Donne by George Peele Maister of artes in Oxford." The British Library, London, contains an autograph letter that Peele sent to Lord Burghley, Queen Elizabeth's principal secretary, in January of 1596. The poet enclosed a poem he had written almost twenty years before and asked for some charity because "Longe sicknes havinge so enfeebled me maketh bashfullnes allmost become impudency."[1] These two documents encompass, as well as any two can, the career of a fine but ultimately disappointed writer. George Peele was exceedingly and justly proud of his university education, but his education, his writing for the Lord Mayor's pageant, and the "history of Troy in 500 Verses" that he sent Burghley could not earn him a living in the London of the 1580s and 1590s. Burghley filed the letter, as David Horne says, "with others from cranks and crackpots," and Peele was dead by the next November.[2]

Talent and Social Class

George Peele belonged to the group an historian has dubbed the "generation of 1560"—a glittering crew of adventurers, politicians, noblemen, and of course, poets and dramatists.[3] Sir Philip Sidney and Robert Devereux, second earl of Essex, were perhaps its most glamorous members, and their literary peers responded enthusiastically to that glamour in dedications, hymns of praise, and songs of mourning. Despite the Elizabethan admiration for Sidney and Essex and despite the fame of such artists as Marlowe and Shakespeare and John Lyly, the last two decades of the sixteenth century (when Peele and the others sought to make their marks) proved complicated and often inhospitable times. The problems can be explained as variously as there are individuals who suffered them and modern scholars to study them, but a few features stand almost beyond question. First, there existed far more talent and far more ambitious talent than society could absorb and put to full use. That is, more talent than careers open to talent. Second and closely related, economic reward more and more became the measure of success even as it came to be more and more the preserve of careers quite foreign to the training and expectations of such men as Sir Walter Ralegh and Essex, or in more humble and different ways, Lyly and Peele and Robert Greene. Various forms of capitalistic risk-taking were splendidly rewarded, but chivalric, martial action was not so certainly compensated. Nor was artistic activity. Indeed, it might be argued that the literary glorification of a Sidney or an Essex, a John Norris or a Francis Drake, was partly the consequence of the writers' frustration, a frustration which often enough echoed their heroes' own.

The career of James Peele, the dramatist's father, is an instructive case. A man of some learning and a member of the Salters' Company, James Peele wrote an important book on "advanced" accounting techniques, worked as a bookkeeper, earned money writing semi-literary material for the annual Lord Mayor's pageants, and eventually achieved a very satisfactory position as Clerk of a London charity-home and school, Christ's Hospital.[4] He also taught in the school and, for a time, conducted a private school of his own. The playwright's father, then, was a tradesman by social class, but also what the Elizabethans would call a "clerk," an educated man with a position which rewarded mental rather than manual work. Understandably enough, James sought to give George greater advantages than he himself enjoyed. He sent his son to Oxford. In doing so, he virtually insured that George Peele would find himself a social amphibian, because Oxford and Cambridge were themselves "in transition," seeking an educational and cultural equilibrium between their older function as training grounds for the clergy and their new status as, seemingly, an avenue to the top (for sons of the middle class) and finishing schools (for sons of the gentry and aristocracy).[5]

The Universities and Literary Careers

While far from exhausted as ideals, the humanist beliefs which had fired the universities in Henry VIII's day and early in Elizabeth's reign no longer matched up with society's capacities or its own self-conception. Where once an M.A. might almost guarantee a satisfactory position in the state bureaucracy or in some great man's household or in the church, there was no longer such assurance because more people were seeking a largely fixed number of places.[6] Of the university-trained men who needed to earn their own livings (rather than enjoy a family fortune or reap the rewards of family influence), few could find places which allowed them either to exercise that training or satisfy the expectations they had discovered (or, effectively, been promised) at the university. Mark Curtis views the mingling of classes at the universities optimistically: it contributed "to a mutuality of outlook and feeling among all important segments of English society," and the students "were bound together by an outlook and attitude which the common features of their education engendered."[7] An anonymous contemporary could sing "Come rich, come poor, come all good wit unto the Muses' mart / Rejoice we Oxford students all."[8] Yet the psychological consequences of ambitious expectation defeated could be just as severe as the social homogeneity Curtis envisions might be fortunate.

Admissions to Oxford and Cambridge slumped markedly between 1590 and 1615, and an "excess of supply over demand" has been proposed as a likely explanation.[9] The problem of a surplus of educated men grew worse rather than better in the years after Peele's death. Speaking specifically of the clergy in 1611, Lord Chancellor Ellesmere worried about the social consequences of too few clerical positions: "I think that we have more need of better livings for learned men than of learned men for these livings, for learning without living doth but breed traitors as common experience too well sheweth."[10] Peele was no traitor, but his letter to Burghley in 1596 shows him a forlorn and disappointed aspirant to success.

One scholar finds that the majority of Elizabethans who hoped to live by their pens were "children of tradesmen . . . from urban rather than agricultural backgrounds."[11] Even if this generalization may be too broad (and it explicitly excludes dramatists), it is safe to say that almost every nonaristocratic Elizabethan writer of any fame needed, hoped for, and sought some source of income other than his creative productions. G. K. Hunter has dissected both the social context and its personal implications for Peele's near-contemporary, John Lyly, a superior dramatist who was at Oxford a year or so ahead of Peele.[12] Lyly's career cannot have been a satisfying one, but he certainly had more advantages—and more success—than Peele. Where Lyly's father has been described as a yeoman "whose wealth and degree of cultivation had raised him into the class of the landed gentry,"[13] Peele belonged to a social stratum at the very least one rung lower. That lower status meant, above all, a much more restricted circle of influential friends and the inescapable need to earn whatever living there was to be earned. It was a maxim of literary, no less than political or military, reward that "Preferment goes by letter and affection," as Shakespeare's Iago bitterly put it. In 1575, four years after Peele went up to Oxford, William Stafford wrote: "Nowadays, when men send their sons to the University, they suffer them no longer to tarry there than to have a little of the Latin tongue, and then they take them away and bestow them to be clerks with some man of law, or some auditor or receiver, or to be a secretary with some great man or other, and so to come to a living."[14] Peele could look for no more help from his family than the education which it must have cost them dear to provide, and he could count on no tailor-made future as a secretary in the government or in some great man's entourage. Indeed, he had no natural allies and that, in turn, meant no natural audience or customers for his talent.

Yet, Peele's background and education made him ambitious and encouraged the belief that the world (or at least the government and the great men at court) owed him a living. That living was not offered him. In its place, Peele chose to exploit his training and talent and become a professional writer. Doing so, he confronted some paradoxical choices. Original, imaginative, nondramatic literature of any great artistic pretension was the preserve of the Court and its satellite, dependent poets. That milieu regarded publication as unworthy, unnecessary, and gauche.[15] Moreover, patronage paid better than print. Alas, poets outnumbered patrons, as Peele's Prologue to *The Honour of the Garter* makes painfully clear, and he appears to have been quite unsuccessful in finding patrons. Alternative sources of income were few: the theater; civic corporations; the Court acting through the Office of the Revels or some other basically propagandistic arm; the stationers (the book trade) with their constant demand for broadsides, news-sheets, and the trashy ballads and pamphlets of an Anthony Munday or (in his own estimate) a Thomas Nashe.[16]

Training which fitted Peele to translate a Greek drama or to write elegant imitations of Latin literature while still at Oxford hardly prepared him to satisfy the paying customers of the London literary world. And yet, if he were to survive, it was just such an audience he had to find. His education was not, of course, wasted. He did occasionally have an opportunity to write for courtly and aristocratic audiences, and his learning marks even the most popular works as those of a "University Wit." Moreover, distinctions among his various clients cannot be drawn too sharply. When he wrote a Lord Mayor's pageant for the very bourgeois trade guilds of London, his classical knowledge stood him in good stead, as did his rhetorical training and many other abilities honed at the university. Still, the lurid bombast of *The Battle of Alcazar,* ripe for Shakespeare's mockery in *2 Henry IV,* appealed to an audience very different from the one which enjoyed the elegant mythological fable of *The Araygnement of Paris* or, for that matter, an audience very different from the one which admired the biblical lyricism of *David and Bethsabe.*

The problems Peele faced can be formulated another way. His two great loves, according to many historians and critics, were pastoralism and patriotism, or the lyric and the jingoistic.[17] But these two "loves" are not really compatible, any more than the love of humane letters and practical politics proved to be at Elizabeth's court. Whether Peele ever consciously realized that his evident interests were irremediably sundered is not an issue, or at least not an issue that can be resolved. A little publication from almost the middle of his professional career neatly illustrates the social, political, and economic crises virtually every member of his generation faced. In 1589, Peele published the ringing and rather good *Farewell to . . . Norris and . . . Drake,* two military heroes off to battle the Spaniards. The poem triumphantly sings England's military glory, her naval ambitions, her past and future exploits—all in seventy-six lines. No matter how drunk with victory and nationalism, the hard-headed London book-buyer could not be expected to purchase such a tiny publication, and something was needed to eke out the "book." Peele provided a poem, *A Tale of Troy,* which apparently dates from almost a decade before, when he was still living at Oxford. Perhaps the military subject matter was a sufficient link to make the union a plausible commercial venture, but intellectually and emotionally the two poems could hardly be further apart. The Trojan poem treats a typical academic topic, just as the Trojan War was a typical academic subject of debate and literary exercise. The poet's splintered desires and abilities appear very clearly: on the one hand, a chauvinistic, war-mongering paean; on the other, a deliberate, slightly archaic celebration of gods and goddesses, mythic heroes, and very literary subjects.

The point is not that each of Peele's efforts could only be appreciated by sharply defined—and different—groups in Elizabethan London. Rather, Peele's canon shows a remarkable formal variety, and very often those diverse forms carry with them equally disparate expectations and audiences. While any given Londoner would be most unlikely to enjoy *The Araygnement of Paris,* a Lord Mayor's pageant, and *David and Bethsabe* equally, there were doubtless some who could appreciate large portions of Peele's output: his public theater plays and his pageants might appeal to one group, and his court plays and his celebration of the Order of the Garter to another. The implied audiences for Peele's works and their manifestly varied contexts nonetheless bring us back to the central point: he sought to satisfy a wide range of tastes because he hoped to open a wide range of purses.

Peele's Canon, Economics, and Culture

If this sketch of the social, economic, and cultural conditions Peele faced when he came to London around 1581 is approximately accurate, then a valuable way into his work would be to identify how the works respond to those contemporary conditions. As a professional writer interested in satisfying the prejudices and preconceptions of his widely varied audiences, Peele offers us a chance to observe a working Elizabethan writer whose literary product owes less to the artist's own individual nature than it does to the corporate natures of the audiences he sought to entertain. While a Marlowe or a Shakespeare or a Jonson might hope both to entertain and to leave a strong personal impression upon the entertainment, a lesser artist (and, perhaps, a needier one) will only intermittently manage the double accomplishment. More often, that lesser artist will offer a clear picture of the moment, the place, the people present, and leave a much hazier impression of his own personality or principles or idiosyncratic concerns. It is often the fate—and the glory—of the minor artist, or the "popular" artist in a very positive sense, to evoke his culture and his historical moment more vividly than the greater figure who creates not for an age, but for all time.

Peele did, of course, have scope for his own interests: few audiences and few occasions so severely stipulate their entertainment that the artist has no room for maneuver. Peele is no exception, and it is possible to uncover certain subjects—the importance of poetry itself, for example—and certain attitudes—patriotism and Protestantism, for example—which appear to be personally important to him and are memorably embodied in his art. Yet, the bias will always lean toward the occasion and the audience and the historical moment. This bias offers a wonderful opportunity to see what being a professional writer might have meant in Elizabethan London and to see what that extraordinarily diverse society found diverting.

Peele apparently found his first audience while still at Oxford. Recitation, imitation, and performance of classical, especially Latin, plays formed a staple of Elizabethan grammar-school education and were probably part of Peele's studies at Christ's Hospital.[18] Early training apparently led to dramatic translation at Oxford. A friend and fellow student, William Gager, wrote two Latin poems entitled "To the Iphigenia translated into English verse by George Peele" and "To the same."[19] Gager, himself a distinguished Latin dramatist, praises Peele's translation (presumably from Euripides) and declares the value of making classical literature available to those who have neither Greek nor Latin. This play has not survived, but the impulse to employ and domesticate classical literature appears everywhere in Peele's later, independent work. Perhaps Peele translated the play as part of his studies, or for fun; perhaps he wrote it for a college performance, since Christ Church had a long history of college drama.[20] Whatever the motivation, this Iphigenia play shows Peele's early interest, his ability, his leaning toward a learned art, and—perhaps—the beginnings of his attempt to please an audience.

Evidently, he gained a reputation as a good man for a play because the college paid him the very large sum of £20 in May 1583 "in respect of the playes & intertaynemt of the palatine laskie."[21] The payment probably reimbursed the former student's expenses as well as rewarding his services. Just what Peele did to earn this sum is unclear, but the occasion is not. The Count Palatine of Siradia (Poland), Albert Alasco, traveled through England from April to September of 1583 and visited Oxford in June. There he saw numerous entertainments, including two plays by William Gager presented at Christ Church. Oxford and Cambridge entertained the queen and various distinguished foreigners lavishly.[22] In Robert Greene's *Friar Bacon and Friar Bungay* (ca. 1591), a group of Oxford dons prepares to receive "all the western potentates," and they agree, "We must lay plots of stately tragedies, / Strange comic shows. . . ."[23] Greene's characters may have been thinking of plays only, but the entertainments traditionally also included orations by important scholars, displays of learning by the students, fireworks, songs, and all the varied pastimes which the queen herself enjoyed when she visited a nobleman's country estate. Even the plays were embroidered with slightly digressive episodes and effects; Gager's *Dido,* presented before Alasco, included a pack of hunting dogs, an artificial snowstorm, and, more conventionally, the descent of various deities from heaven.[24]

After receiving the M.A. in 1579, Peele remained in Oxford for about two years, marrying a local woman and engaging in an elaborate and typically Elizabethan series of lawsuits to gain her substantial patrimony. The fact that his college apparently summoned him back to help entertain Alasco suggests several things: he continued his friendships with members of Christ Church; he had earned, or enhanced, a reputation for drama; and—perhaps—he had gained experience in pleasing an aristocratic audience. Certainly by 1584, the year after the Oxford entertainment, Peele had written *The Araygnement of Paris,* a pastoral play performed before Queen Elizabeth and her court.[25] This first surviving dramatic effort substantiates the talents Peele's college associates wanted for the Alasco celebrations: it has many similarities to such shows. Alongside this courtly success, or perhaps because of it, Peele gained the great London livery companies as clients. He supplied the civic equivalents of a courtly "show" by writing at least two (and probably more) pageants for the Lord Mayor's annual installation ceremony and parade. Peele's skills made pageant-writing congenial as well as profitable, and he seems to have been following a family tradition.[26]

At the end of the decade, Peele again evidences his eagerness to cash in on current events and popular reactions to them. After the Armada's failure in 1588, enthusiasm for some sort of punitive action ran high, and Sir Francis Drake and Sir John Norris were dispatched to attack the Iberian peninsula. Despite Queen Elizabeth's prohibition, her current favorite, the earl of Essex, also joined the naval and military force. The expedition proved a dismaying failure, but as we have seen, Peele cheerfully sang its departure in *A Farewell . . . to . . . Norris and . . . Drake* and just as jingoistically welcomed Essex home in *An Eglogue Gratulatorie*. Without question, his own feelings contributed to the poet's enthusiasm, but it is hard to doubt that potential book-buyers' patriotism had as large a share as private conviction. In the 1590s, the playwright's flair for pageantry, his interest in courtly and civic audiences, and his need for money all join to produce several poems documenting various aristocratic occasions which also involved large and popular processions.

Just when Peele began writing for the heterogeneous public theater audiences is unknown. Aside from *The Araygnement of Paris*, all the plays generally considered his work—*The Old Wives Tale, David and Bethsabe, The Battle of Alcazar*, and *Edward I*—appear to have been designed for performance by the great companies of adult actors who dominated the professional stage in the late 1580s and early 1590s. Although *The Old Wives Tale* has many intriguing hints of some other auspices, its title page attributes it to the Queen's Men, and *The Battle of Alcazar* (again according to the title page) belonged to the Admiral's Men. Philip Henslowe, impresario and landlord for the Admiral's Men, recorded a play which may be *Edward I;* and despite certain features which recall the private (children's) theater, *David and Bethsabe* was also probably part of an adult company's repertory. Many other plays or parts of plays have been attributed to Peele; in fact, with the possible exception of Robert Greene, he has the dubious distinction of being claimed as the true father of more dramatic foundlings than any other Elizabethan dramatist.[27]

The temptation to assign Peele various anonymous plays is understandable. While certain literary and dramatic elements appear throughout his known canon, it remains diverse enough to accept an addition or two. In fact, none of his immediate contemporaries produced anything like the same diversity while achieving an equal artistic level, although younger writers (Dekker and Middleton, for example) are instructive parallels. The single unifying element appears to be an economic one: Peele wrote to earn money. He served many different markets and many different masters. Given our knowledge, it is impossible to be certain why Peele chose to write. Talent, education, pride, and even political conviction must have played their parts. Despite his fairly large and varied output, Peele probably could not have survived on his literary earnings alone. Few contemporaries of his kind did. Marlowe, Jonson, and Shakespeare all had other sources of income, and two of them could rely on some fairly substantial, if intermittent, help from aristocratic patrons. Robert Greene and Thomas Nashe lived miserable existences trying to survive through what Nashe called the "endeavors of art"; they became—temporarily at least—hacks and even the virtual slaves of their miserly bookseller-employers. One reason Peele survived financially must have been his first wife's inheritance. It amounted to at least £250, or roughly twelve years' salary for James Peele.[28] Perhaps the inheritance, or distaste, or lack of ability kept Peele from writing prose fictions and pamphlets. In any case, neither inherited capital nor literary earnings staved off poverty if we believe—and there is no reason to doubt—his letter to Burghley.

To see Peele's writing as an economic as well as a cultural phenomenon offers us a rewarding and perhaps novel view of an early professional writer. This artist sought to please in order to live. His work's enduring beauty argues more than chameleon adaptability, although it is hard to distinguish precisely the shares of cultural or political conditioning, economic necessity, and personal or artistic conviction. In any event, he fits very well the condescending remark of Ben Jonson's Sir John Daw, a pseudowit who would not defile himself by writing for money: "Why, every man that writes in verse is not a poet; you have of the Wits that write verses and yet are no poets; they are poets that live by it, the poor fellows that live by it."[29] Peele tried to live by it.

Chapter Two

Entertainments for Court and City

Public ceremony, festival, show, the drama of street and hall, village green and innyard, permeated Elizabethan life. Many of these events were deliberately, if subtly, political. Ruled and ruling classes expressed their loyalty, their power, and their sense of community in ways generally foreign to modern nation states, especially those states which emphasize the individual rather than a group as the fundamental social unit. A modern citizen's allegiance may still employ public totems—the eagle, lion, or bear, for example—but the emblems have neither a vital connection with a single individual leader nor the power to evoke unified and delimited ideas, attitudes, and meanings. In Elizabethan society—a society divided over religion, the distribution of political authority, and indeed the state's very definition—images of power and ceremonies of mutual responsibility asserted, and even seemed to "prove," the existence of a splendidly reassuring universal order.[1] Court drama, city pageant, and the renewal or invention of medieval and pseudo-medieval public ceremonies all worked to announce and exploit the public values essential for public harmony. Thus, a great deal of what today appears to have been independently conceived "literature" or "art" served also, perhaps even primarily, as propaganda.

Elizabethan patrons might not have stipulated the philosophical and political programs of their artistic employees with quite the tenacity or rigor of Italian princes, but they could trust the power of convention and the purse to "guide" and shape that artistic product. Moreover, the hired artist (like Peele or Lyly) and the amateur one (like Sidney) almost certainly shared the patrons' values and ambitions, at least in general.[2] Consequently, a substantial body of literary and subliterary works promoted various public myths, national self-conceptions, and the half-begged, half-demanded desires of many different social groups. Courtly recreation became not only a recognized way to affirm larger social, political, and religious values, but also a means to promote specific policies and to advance specific individuals.[3] Eager, ambitious, and poor, Peele attempted to supply what his society seemed to want. At the start of his professional career, he offered *The Araygnement of Paris* to the court and sometime later contrived *The Old Wives Tale,* possibly for a similar audience. He also sold his talents to others, individual and corporate. Like his father before him, he tapped an important middle-class and mercantile vein by writing pageants for the annual installation of London's Lord Mayor, and he exploited some of Elizabeth's most successful minglings of honor and publicity, the elaborately revitalized Knights of the Garter and the annual tournaments celebrating her accession to the throne. This chapter examines Peele's works deliberately tailored to specific courtly and civic occasions, the Accession Day tilts, the Lord Mayor's pageants, and the Garter installation ceremony. These occasional poems provide an excellent context for two of Peele's finest dramatic works, *The Araygnement of Paris* and *The Old Wives Tale,* the subjects of the next chapters.

Accession Day Poems

The tilts, or jousts, which marked the anniversary of Elizabeth's accession, 17 November, were the most spectacular regular public events of the period. Shortly after the day had been established as the year's most significant secular holiday, that is, from the early or mid-1570s, the annual events became elaborate and costly extravaganzas. Roy Strong describes them as "a marriage of the arts in the service of Elizabethan state-craft," a phrase which describes virtually every major form of court revel.[4] Like other entertainments, the Tiltyard shows served as coded exchanges between subjects and sovereign. Through his choice of armor, supporting cast, and allegorical decoration—for example, the riddling visual motifs painted on his shield—a nobleman could protest, palliate, request, or advocate some royal action or reaction. Other tilters might amplify, or challenge, that "speech" to the queen, and she, in turn, might respond very bluntly or join in the allusive symbolic conversation.

Polyhymnia (1590) and *Anglorum Feriae* (1595) record two Accession Day tilts and introduce very clearly some of the "conversational formulae" exchanged by court and monarch. A pastoral and chivalric ambience, for example, or repeated contests requiring the queen to act as an arbiter appear and reappear in the tilts, in the country-house entertainments which Elizabeth saw on her frequent progresses, and *mutatis mutandis* in *The Araygnement of Paris* and many other works of court literature. Just as the country-house entertainments became individually and collectively "a . . . serial . . . in which courtiers cast themselves in whatever rôle suited the moment and their plea,"[5] so too, the tilts apparently develop a slightly disjointed continuous story. This continuity of material and political design appears in all forms of court entertainment and literature. Thus, the "pastoral preoccupation" of the country-house revels and the Tiltyard pageants passes—in demonstrably textual ways—into literature as diverse as *The Arcadia,* the lyric poetry of the 1580s, John Lyly's plays, and *The Araygnement of Paris.*[6]

Peele himself first appears as a recorder, rather than inventor, of court festivities in *Polyhymnia,* his account of the 1590 Accession Day tilt. *Polyhymnia* has the chief advantages of an Elizabethan occasional poem—immediacy, a kind of breathless vivacity—and the main disadvantage—a dreary duty to include every event and every participant. Consequently, Peele divides his poem into sections recording (often in no very specific detail) the combats of thirteen pairs of eminent Elizabethans. Sometimes this journalistic determination makes for a "then-and-then-and-then" structure with hardly any individual features to distinguish the parts. Nonetheless, verbal archaisms do catch the "gothick" quality of Elizabethan nobles pretending to be medieval knights:

> Wherefore it fares as whilom and of yore,
> In armour bright and sheene, faire Englands knights
> In honour of their peerelesse Soveraigne:
> . . . .
> Make to the Tylt amaine. . . . (12–14, 16)

This same early passage underlines the tilt's official and very political purpose: honoring Elizabeth (see also lines 78–79, 90–93, and 172). While every Accession Day tilt made a uniform political statement, they permitted many eccentric individual performances and could simultaneously, as in 1590, seem to create an overall theme.

The unofficial and unannounced theme in 1590 might be called "change and continuity." Peele's chief poetic problem was welding thirteen different but virtually indistinguishable pseudomedieval pseudocombats into some sort of coherence. He took his clue from the 1590 tilt's most prominent event, the retirement of Sir Henry Lee as Queen's Champion, and from the tilt's most extravagant individual display, the earl of Essex's appearance, "all in Sable sad" (98), mourning Sir Philip Sidney's death. Using Cumberland's succession to Lee and Essex's replacement (matrimonial and political) of Sidney, Peele refers the changes within unchanging patterns to the queen herself, *semper eadem,* always the same. To distinguish one pair of combatants from another, Peele chose to emphasize the contrasting colors of their armor and the variety of heraldic detail each combatant bore on his shield.

This emphasis upon appearance—the colors, emblematic details, the order and number of participants—makes *Polyhymnia* a fascinating record of Elizabethan society amid its serious pastimes and reminds us that the slightest detail in such events almost certainly had a significance. Thus, even when Peele cannot explain something, he assumes it has an interpretation: ". . . gentle Gerrarde, all in white and greene, / Collours (belike) best serving his conceit" (56–57).[7] More often, of course, the details of appearance could be explained. Lee's "Caparison charg'd with Crownes, / Oreshadowed with a withered running Vine" (22–23) represents the aged Champion's retirement, and "the golden Eagle" Lord Ferdinando Strange bore was the "Stanleyes olde Crest and honourable badge" (40–41). The choice and use of some costly and often enigmatic emblem or more elaborate decorative scheme pleasantly puzzles the spectators and compliments the sovereign; thus, Peele found William Knowles, "in his plumes, his colours and device, / Expressing Warriors wit and Courtiers grace" (179–80).

Peele's determination to record the tilt's visual aspects produces detailed accounts of the knights' ceremonial entries. Some tilters simply rode into the yard, saluted the queen, and approached the barriers to fight. More costly and elaborate equipment would include a "pageant," or horse-drawn wagon, carrying the tilter and his symbolically clad servants, the tilting horses and armor (usually painted or adorned with emblematic designs), and finally a "Trounchman" (47), or interpreter, to explain the symbolism and present the knight, who then "Dismountes him from his pageant" (50). The "shows" and "devices" often seem like vivified illustrations from contemporary emblem books.[8] Robert Cary entered with a common emblem, a heart surrounded by flames, probably painted on his shield or a scroll (lines 154–58), and Anthony Cooke offers other images familiar from emblem books (lines 189–93). If allegorical interpretations were easy, so were classical and mythological analogies: Robert Knowles appears "with golden boughes" (probably his lances, or perhaps some image on shield or armor), "Entring the listes like Tytan, arm'd with fire, / When in the queachy plot Python he slew" (211–13) and Thomas Sidney "So well behav'd himselfe . . . As Paris had to great Achilles Launce / Applied his tender fingers and his force" (242–44).

The most extravagant "show" of the tilt belonged to the earl of Essex and commemorated the friend, Philip Sidney, whose widow Essex had married and whose political and "mythological" heir he hoped to be.[9] Peele carefully surrounds the central event with details of other tilters' bright, contrasting colors—red and green for Lord Burgh and Edward Denny, Lord Strange's gold, "Or and Azure" and "Orenge-tawnie" for Sir Charles Blunt and Thomas Vavasor. The color contrast and a long grammatical suspension which refuses to name the subject intensify the entry's surprise:

> Then proudly shocks amid the Martiall throng,
> Of lustie Lancieres, all in Sable sad,
> Drawen on with cole-blacke Steeds of duskie hue,
> In stately Chariot full of deepe device,
> Where gloomie Time sat whipping on the teame,
> Just backe to backe with this great Champion;
> Yoong Essex, that thrice honorable Earle,
> Yclad in mightie Armes of mourners hue,
> And plume as blacke as is the Ravens wing,
> That from his armour borrowed such a light,
> As bowes of Vu [Yew] receives from shady streame,
> His staves were such, or of such hue at least,
> As are those banner staves that mourners beare,
> And all his companie in funerall blacke,
> As if he mourn'd to thinke of him he mist,
> Sweete Sydney, fairest shepheard of our greene,
> Well lettred Warriour, whose successor he
> In love and Armes had ever vowed to be. (97–114)

Peele's affection for Sidney, mentioned in lines 225–26, and his profound admiration for Essex give this passage an unusual density and attractiveness.[10] Varying hues of black and the pageant's funereal purpose allow two nicely judged similes: the black colors reflect one another as a stream's dark waters reflect the symbolically mournful yew tree, while the banners Essex's servants carry remind Peele of the banners carried in Sidney's own funeral procession. Time hastens us all toward death: first Sidney and now his dear friend making this ceremonial and memorial entry.

Essex's magnificent "device" echoes throughout the poem. Thomas Knollys, a "friend and follower" of Essex, also appears "In mourning Sable dight by simpathie" (201), and Cooke of course portrayed "Life and Death . . . in his show" (189). Despite time's destruction and sorrow's shows, Peele ends his description of the tilt by promising renewal and perpetuation because 17 November is "that golden time . . . the byrth-day of our happinesse, / The blooming time, the spring of Englands peace" (262–64).

After the tilt comes a coda describing Sir Henry Lee's resignation. The elderly knight tells the Queen

> He would betake him to his Oraysons:
> And spend the remnant of his waining age,
> (Unfit for warres and Martiall exploites)
> In praiers for her endlesse happines. (296–99)

Lee then advances Cumberland as his replacement, and Elizabeth (now employing couplets) "seem'd to say,"

> Good Woodman, though thy greene be turn'd to gray,
> Thy age past Aprils prime, and pleasant May:
> Have thy request, we take him [Cumberland] at thy praise,
> May he succeed the honour of thy daies. (301–4)[11]

Age, retirement, and death are not conclusions, but the springs of renewal: "many Champions such may England live to have / And daies and yeares as many such, as she in heart can crave" (308–9). The suddenly longer lines in poulter's measure mimic the extension of Elizabeth's reign "beyond" iambic pentameter, just as the couplet and the ceremony serve to conclude the poem. Change—Sidney's death or Lee's retirement—takes place within a secure frame—the tilt, England's peace, Elizabeth's immutable nature—which provides continuity.

Peele's poem celebrating the tilt of 1595, *Anglorum Feriae,* survives only in an autograph manuscript dedicated to Katherine, countess of Huntingdon.[12] Peele may have chosen the countess because she was Northumberland's daughter and therefore a potential source of reward as her father had been for *The Honour of the Garter* (1593). Given the poem's character, however, a political explanation is also possible. The countess's husband, Henry Hastings, third earl, was Lord President of the North until his death on 14 December 1595 and a strong Puritan and noted priest-hunter.[13] Intense patriotism and Protestant sympathies would be appropriate in the dedicatee because the poem is more topical than *Polyhymnia* and much less detailed in its description of the tilt's events. In fact, the tilt is first mentioned at line 163, almost halfway through the poem. The opening sections hardly prepare the reader for the second half. Instead, a series of blank-verse paragraphs, each ending in a couplet, reviews Queen Elizabeth's career and defines her place in English society and English hearts.

Behind the extravagant praise of Elizabeth and equally extravagant condemnation of England's foes, one senses how radically Peele's poetic program has changed since he wrote *Polyhymnia.* That change arises from the social, political, and religious crises which had forced themselves on public attention in the five years since *Polyhymnia.* In 1590, the queen, the court, and the people were still united in the aftermath of the Armada. Or if they were not entirely in accord, they could nonetheless be portrayed that way, as Peele does in *A Farewell . . . to . . . Norris and . . . Drake* (1589). Essex might mourn Sidney, and the spectators sympathize, but there was little reason to doubt—again, publicly—that the future would be any different from or any worse than the past. Without straining the facts unacceptably, *Polyhymnia* could envision an almost immutable aristocratic and royal future, effortlessly resisting foreign and native threats. The period between 1590 and 1595 had, however, made that vision much less certain. Essex's own efforts to advance himself and his friends, his intemperance, and his glamour had all begun to disturb the courtly and political balance which the older generation of Elizabethan politicians and aristocrats had forged. Many of the great names were gone: Leicester, Walsingham, Hatton. In their place appeared men not less able, but less adept at cloaking self-interest in public duty.

If the court began to seem a less secure place, so too did other areas of society. The festering problem of religious schism—the challenge to central authority posed by both radical Protestantism and clandestine Roman Catholicism—now produced serious and very public threats. These difficulties had surfaced before, in the Babington conspiracy to free Mary Queen of Scots, for example, and earlier in the revolt of various Roman Catholic nobles, but religious issues now found a twin focus: the problem of Elizabeth's successor and Parliament's outspoken desire for religious reform. Whispers and more than whispers of Spanish-sponsored plots against Elizabeth's life reached the government. On slender evidence and perhaps chiefly to feed Essex's *amour propre,* the queen's physician, Roderigo Lopez, was executed for conspiring to poison her. Other plots and other conspirators, some madcap and some deadly, were uncovered.[14] Exiled English Roman Catholics bombarded their co-religionists with propaganda from various Continental towns and seminaries and sent many priests into England secretly. The poet-priest Robert Southwell, for example, was arrested, tortured, and executed in February 1595, and another Jesuit, Robert Parsons, helped to write the seditious *Conference about the next Succession,* arguing the Spanish claim on the English throne. The book began to circulate in England around September of 1595.[15]

Religious belief and political activity went hand in hand among the more radical Protestants, too. Peter Wentworth repeatedly (and loyally) raised troublesome issues of Parliament's independence, of the Church's organization, and of the need to determine Elizabeth's successor before her death. Wentworth and a number of like-minded men went to the Tower for their pains, and Parliament was obliged to pass the last and in some ways most stringent religious legislation of the period, the "Act to retain the Queen Majesty's subjects in their due obedience" (1593).[16]

All these upheavals and more define the context of *Anglorum Feriae.* Doubtless each separate problem had appeared in the past, often decades in the past, but in 1595 it was certainly possible to feel—as Peele apparently did—that many single troubles had begun to unite into battalions. Such a conviction makes the poem's tone and structure explicable. Before reaching his nominal subject, the tilt, Peele invokes the muse of history, Clio, "sagest of these sisters nine," and invites her to "Elizaes Coort, Astraeas earthlie heaven" (6, 8). The verbal repetition which marks the poem's first half soon appears: "Write write you Cronicles of Tyme and Fame, / Elizabeth by miracles preserved" (17–18). The next three verse paragraphs record Elizabeth's life before the coronation (55–74), her anointed accession to "hir kingly Fathers seate" (75–93), and London's special love, the "holy tunes and sacrifize of thankes, / Englandes Metropolis as incense sendes" (94–113). Loyal and well-written as each paragraph is, the poem becomes almost a guide to the tilt's propagandistic, metaphorical, and political meanings. *Anglorum Feriae* analyzes values.

The gaudy trappings which fill *Polyhymnia* are not entirely forgotten, of course. Clio and her sisters (or perhaps all Englishwomen) must become emblematic Tudors: "weare Eglantine / And wreathes of Roses red and white" (39–40). Despite the rustic touches—"Lovely Shepherdes" dance "alonge the chaulkie clyffes of Albion" (43–44)—the day's true tenor cannot be long ignored: "Clio recorde howe shee hathe bin preserved / Even in the gates of deathe and from hir youthe, / to govern Englande in the waies of Truthe" (56–58). Religious allusions emphasize the special Providence which guards England and equally stress Elizabeth's personal importance to her people's faith.[17] Mention of religious schism naturally prompts thoughts of Henry VIII, who founded the national church, and of foreign religious enemies. Peele lightly omits Edward VI and Mary in order to place Henry's "massie scepter and that swoorde / that awed the worlde" (78–79) directly in his younger daughter's hand. These instruments have driven "the daringe foe / back to his Den . . . weried with wars by lande and wrack by sea" (81–83); thus England's escape from the Armada and her more equivocal military successes in France and the Low Countries are made to confirm the nation's faith and Elizabeth's right to rule.

Peele meets the twin issues of religion and succession more openly in the paragraph following the personification of "Londons Shepherde Gardian." Abstract loyalty becomes concrete: "in sympathie and sweete accorde / all loyall subjects joine" (114–15). More specifically yet, Elizabeth's subjects give thanks for

> . . . That day whereon this Queen
> inaugured was and hollyly installd
> anointed of the highest kinge of kinges
> in hir hereditarie royall righte
> successively to sit enthronized. . . . (120–24)

The passage sounds like a contribution to the pamphlet warfare over the succession. Such phrases as "hollyly installd" and "hereditarie royall righte" are not complimentary small coins, but the language of political controversy and crisis. Polemic surges through the personification of "pale Envie" which flees England "to murmur that abroade / hee durst not openly disgorge at home" (130–31). "Envy" of course is that body of English Roman Catholics who undertook to minister to the spiritual needs of their fellows in England and in so doing "revolt from their allegeance" (140). Freed of their duty to Elizabeth by the papal bull which excommunicated her, these men are "condemned amonge the Turkes and infidells" (142). Invited by Catholic propaganda to overthrow the English government, they become "false Architects of . . . bloodie stratagems" (143, 145) and "cruell seige they laie unto hir life" (146).

The near hysteria and lurid language contrast markedly with Peele's usual poise and often rather pallid diction. However uncharacteristic, this violent outburst forms the poem's logical hinge. Now, at last, we reach the tilters who are introduced as a "troupe of Loyall English knightes . . . reddy to do their Duties . . . against the mightiest enemie shee [Elizabeth] hathe" (159, 164, 165). After renegade traitors, a representative band of true knights and true Englishmen appears. Their leader, of course, is the earl of Cumberland, the man who replaced Sir Henry Lee as "Knighte of the crowne" (173), and Peele alludes gracefully to the family seat, Pendragon Castle: "his Holde / Kept by a Dragon laden with faire spoiles" (175–76). Although Peele just manages to include the names of all twenty participants, *Anglorum Feriae* gives much less detail of the tilt than *Polyhymnia*. There remain obligatory references to classical myth and heroes (e.g., "K[ing] Priams Valeant sonnes" in line 266), but romance references predominate. *Polyhymnia* described the sons of Francis Knollys as "Horatii" or the sons of "olde Duke Aymon," an allusion to *Les Quatre Fils Aymon,* a French romance. *Anglorum Feriae* exploits medieval legend and romance more frequently. Peele makes a typical romance pun on Sir James Skidmore's name, just as Spenser seems to do: "Le Scu d'Amour: The armes of Loialtie / lodgd Skydmore in his harte" (319–20).[18] Shakespeare's patron, the earl of Southampton, recalls an earlier hero: "South Hampton ran / as Bevis of South Hampton that good knighte" (227–28). More British legend appears with Knollys's three sons: "they showed as were K[ing] Arthures knightes / he whilom usd to feast at Camilot" (264–65). Although the tilt's pseudomedievalism may domesticate these allusions, the contemporary threat of foreign aggression makes native hero-worship more apt in 1595 than it would have been in 1590. Even more than *Polyhymnia, Anglorum Feriae* stresses tradition, England's ancient peace, and the monarchy's long history.

Five years have not changed Essex's character, and once again he has the grandest show. Renowned for both "wisdome in his younger yeares / and Love to armes" (192–93), Essex enters apparelled in appropriate Tudor colors, "white and faire carnacion" (191). A contemporary observer wrote that Essex's device was "much commended," as well it might be since Francis Bacon apparently wrote most of it.[19] Having entered the Tiltyard, Essex met three representative figures: a hermit, a Secretary (or politician), and a Soldier. An interpreter's speech explained that each figure "sollicited diversly" (196) the earl, urging their respective careers. Although Peele politely comments that any choice Essex makes "shall his nobilitie become" (205), the knowledgeable spectator could hardly miss the hint that Essex was uncertain about how to direct his energies. Given his past military escapades and his intense efforts to become politically indispensable to Elizabeth, the show might also hold the threat of independent, rebellious action or (equally disobedient) a refusal to participate in public life if his desires were unsatisfied. The queen and many courtiers would know, moreover, that Essex had recently suffered two notable defeats in his attempts to win Bacon high legal office: first Coke became Attorney General and then, only twelve days before the tilt, Fleming gained the Solicitor General's post. Essex had supported Bacon's candidacy for both.[20] Thus, the public ceremony which expressed so many royal attitudes and values once again served to expound a personal crisis as well. Essex's little psychomachia had a happy ending. At the banquet following the tilt, a page delivered a speech declaring that Elizabeth's service surpassed and combined the alternatives Essex had faced in the Tiltyard. According to Rowland Whyte, the queen was bored that evening, but others—especially Essex's colleagues on the Privy Council—must have been relieved that this ambitious and unpredictable nobleman professed fidelity, at least for now.

After the intensely anxious tone of the first half, *Anglorum Feriae* settles into a more documentary mode. Only Essex's show implicitly reminds us of political maneuver and ambition. The festival itself reassures the poet, just as it aimed to reassure the spectators. Ceremonial order, loyal jousting, the queen's life-giving powers—all these qualities balance and overcome the fears of assassination, of foreign attack, and of religious discord which fill the poem's opening. At the very end, however, Peele's obligatory prayer for perpetual happiness once more edges from hyperbole into near hysteria:

> Longe may they run in honor of the Day
> Longe may shee live to do them honors right
> to grace their sportes and them as shee hath donne
> Englands Astraea Albions shininge Sunne.
> and may shee shine in beautie freshe and sheene
> Hundreds of yeares our thrice renowmed queen. (328–33)

To hope that the sixty-three-year-old Elizabeth might reign for "Hundreds of yeares" is unnecessarily fatuous. Even a poem tied to the rules of flattery could avoid such inelegant excess, just as it could avoid the triple repetition of "write." Once again, contemporary dangers frighten the poet, and he retreats into formula, almost incantation. Within the grand display itself, a spectator might find Essex's device a troubling hint of instability. In 1601, two of the day's tilters would die as rebels against their queen. *Anglorum Feriae* is probably Peele's last surviving work, and like his other writings it mirrors his increasingly apprehensive and fragmented society.

Lord Mayor's Pageants

The two poems on the Accession Day tilts have both literary and historical value. *Anglorum Feriae* especially is a fine occasional poem, and together the poems are also the fullest surviving accounts of these important events. Peele's scripts, or scenarios, for pageants marking the annual installations of London's Lord Mayors have some remarkable parallels with the tilt poems. "The Device of the Pageant Borne before Wolstan Dixi" (1585) is the first complete surviving text for such an occasion, and *Descensus Astraeae* (1591) is the first to have its own title and therefore to claim a place as an independent creative work rather than as a piece of civic public relations.[21] The parallels extend beyond coincidence. The Dixi pageant is a simple praise of London and Elizabeth and their mutual loyalty and affection. In it, Peele describes a relation between citizen and queen very like the relation between noble and queen in *Polyhymnia,* and the pageant's emotive moments resurface in the fervent passage devoted to London in *Anglorum Feriae.* With *Descensus Astraeae,* however, he approaches the more ambiguous atmosphere of *Anglorum Feriae*'s overt political and social commentary. These similarities arise from Peele's own preoccupations and from the fact that the Lord Mayor's pageants were the civic equivalent of various court entertainments.[22] Consequently, both forms often employ similar tactics to praise and admonish the spectators or to debate contemporary issues.

London's Lord Mayors were selected from the members of her twelve great livery companies, or guilds, and the inauguree's company spent large sums of money on the public procession which welcomed their member on the day of his installation, 29 October. Great care and energy went into selecting the men to write the script (or "device") and to construct the actual pageant itself, carried by porters in the procession.[23] Each company naturally wanted to advertise itself as well as the new Lord Mayor, so the pageants often included references to the company and to the mayor's name. Wolstan Dixi was a member of the Skinners' Company, whose emblem was a lynx or "lucerne." Thus, in the 1585 pageant, the "Presenter" (an interpreter similar to the "Trounch-man" who preceded some knights into the Tiltyard) appears riding on "a Luzarne," probably made of plaster and lath. The procession also typically included "wildmen," legendary giants, devils, and other exotic personages: in 1585, the Presenter was *"apparelled like a Moore."*[24] The Presenter calls the allegorical figures on the pageant "This Emblem" (8) and provides a brief synopsis of their meaning. He emphasizes the "Service of Honour and of Loyaltie" London owes the sovereign and then describes the various figures—a franklin, a farmer, a soldier, and a sailor, for example, along with a "reverend honorable Dame, / Science [Knowledge] the sap of every common wealth" (29–30)—who contribute to London's prosperity and safety. The opening speech advises the new mayor: "This now remaines right honourable Lord, / That carefully you doo attend and Keep, / This lovely Lady [London] rich and beautifull" (43–45).

Now it is the turn of the children seated on the pageant to speak their various pieces. London herself is represented along with "The Thames," "The Cuntry" (that is, London's economic hinterland), "Magnanimity," and "Loyaltie." To distinguish these speeches from the Presenter's blank verse, Peele gives the children varied prosodic forms, usually six-line iambic-pentameter stanzas rhyming *a b a b c c.* The pageant ends with four nymphs, each bearing a lighted torch and praying for Elizabeth's honor and continued happiness. The script does little more than mouth the expected platitudes of congratulation, loyalty, and social interdependence, and it has no "plot" or structure other than a simple honoring of Queen, Lord Mayor, and City.

The same cannot be said for *Descensus Astraeae.* The passage of six years, growing social and political difficulties, and Peele's evident attempt to make the pageant a work of art as well as publicity produce the most sophisticated of the Elizabethan Lord Mayor's pageants. Peele introduces a rudimentary plot concerning the social and political forces arrayed against Queen Elizabeth, and to the morality-abstractions of the Dixi pageant he now adds several figures from classical mythology. Principally, he draws upon the classical myth of "Astraea daughter of the immortall Jove" (14), a shepherdess, according to Peele, who lived on earth during the Golden Age, but when "yron age had kindled cruel warres . . . the thundring Jove, / raught hence this gracious nymph" (67, 70–71) and took her up to heaven. As the title indicates, this pageant will show the return of Astraea to earth, signaling the return of the Golden Age itself. Naturally, there can be no question of Astraea's identity: "heere she sits in beautie fresh and sheene, / Shadowing the person of a peerelesse Queene" (74–75). In short, Elizabeth is Astraea, or as *Anglorum Feriae* puts it: "Englands Astraea Albions shininge Sunne." The primary literary source for the Astraea myth and its pastoral accoutrements is Vergil's Eclogue IV, which many Christian readers interpreted as a prediction of the coming of the Savior.

As the Accession Day tilts and Peele's own *Araygnement of Paris* show, the search for pagan and mythological figures to describe Queen Elizabeth was a general literary preoccupation. That Astraea should appear in a civic pageant, carefully explained for a public which lacked classical training, gives the myth much more than a courtly or purely complimentary value.[25] *Anglorum Feriae* clearly indicates that the 1590s were a period of great anxiety. Worries over the succession, religious controversy, increasing economic difficulties exacerbated by foreign wars and bad harvests, the loss of an older, reassuring generation of senior politicians—all these factors had begun to seep into public ceremonies and festivals. In short, London and England needed the image of Elizabeth-Astraea as much as the court for its own propagandistic and sycophantic purposes also needed that image.

Political and religious issues are at the heart of *Descensus Astraeae.* As the Presenter ends his speech with a catalog of popular leaders—Caesar, Pompey, Alexander, Hector—each of whom contributes some quality to the paragon Elizabeth, he explicitly mentions foreign Protestant friends (at this time, the Dutch and French) who need assistance: "Strengthen thy neighbours, propagate thine owne" (49). Astraea *"with hir sheephook"* (alluding to both the pastoral and Christian meanings of her myth) addresses the London-folk, urging them to "Pay to immortall Jove immortall thankes" (57) for peace and prosperity. The pageant then alternates between the forces of disruption and the allegorical figures who support Elizabeth's reign. Sitting by a fountain on the pageant's platform, *"Superstition. A Friar"* and *"Ignorance. A Priest"* attempt to poison the commonwealth's life-giving well, but Astraea-Elizabeth's glorious chastity holds them rapt and ineffective: "It is in vaine hir eye keepes me in awe" (62). A carefully selected group of pagan, Christian, and chivalric figures now hymns Elizabeth's praises: first the three Graces, then the three theological virtues (Charity, Hope, and Faith), and finally Honor and "Champion." This last figure, perhaps alluding to the Queen's Champion (as in the tilts) or to the giants who often accompanied the pageant, vows to "Breath terror to the proud aspiring foe" (102) and assures Elizabeth she will suffer no harm from the last threatening persons, two "Malecontents." These native enemies admit that they "faint and quaile, / For mightie is the truth and will prevaile" (112–13).[26]

True to her celestial origin, Astraea-Elizabeth surpasses the mundane disputes and protectors we have seen. All nature, time, and fortune concur to "Produce hir yeares to make them numberlesse" (34). Astraea descends to inaugurate a period of happiness and peace in the midst of England's troubles. Peele's show takes a number of contemporary difficulties and blends them into a reassuring pageant. More overtly than most civic pageants, *Descensus Astraeae* uses the materials and expresses the contemporary concerns which also appear in court entertainments.

Occasional Court Poems

Peele's intense patriotism and his political awareness appear throughout the civic pageants, the Accession Day poems, and even the minor poems written to celebrate the departure of Drake and Norris for Portugal or for Essex's return from that ill-starred adventure. Political sympathy, love of nation, and professional ambition all mingle inextricably. Peele offered what his clients wanted, and he wanted what they wanted. In these matters his finest occasional poem, *The Honour of the Garter* (1593), is no different, but Peele now responds to a major political and social event more personally. Although Edward III founded the Order of the Garter about 1344, its ceremonies and especially the crowd-pleasing procession of the knights were revived and developed under the Tudors. Elizabeth made "deliberate use of the Garter to create another Day in honour" of herself and her knights.[27]

The gorgeous ceremonial show of 26 June 1593 obviously intrigued the poet, and he provides a virtual guidebook not only to that particular installation of five men as Knights of the Garter, but to the order's entire history. At the same time, he seeks to honor one man specifically, Henry Percy, ninth earl of Northumberland, who paid him £3 for the poem commemorating his own installation.[28] Northumberland befriended many "artizans and schollers," and his own reputation as a student of "Mathematique skill" and "of Trismegistus and Pythagoras" (Prologue, 6, 8, and 14) earned him the contemporary nickname of "the Wizard Earl." The happy economic fortune of a commission also allowed Peele to frame his poem with a prologue and epilogue speaking directly to Northumberland, the "Muses love, Patrone, and favoret" (Prol., 5), about contemporary poetry. Poetry is in a sorry state. Her patrons, "liberall Sidney, famous for the love / He bare to learning and to Chivalrie; / And vertuous Walsingham" (Prol., 36–38), are dead, and Peele wonders why all the other poets he names have not fled a "world, / That favours Pan and Phoebus both alike" (Prol., 52–53).[29] Only Northumberland remains, a "Heroycall" spirit in "these unhappy times," to support "learning . . . with glorious hands" (Prol., 23–25).

Biased though Peele may be, it is still quite extraordinary to regard literary patronage as the distinguishing mark of "Heroycall spirites." Peele makes a political statement as well as an economic plea or professional observation when he singles out three men eminent for their radicalism—Sidney, Walsingham, and the suspiciously learned and occult-leaning Northumberland. Alongside the prologue's compliments and its age-old cry for more support, there runs a more subtle argument which connects political failings with the collapse of patronage. The only hope for poets left behind in this "Center, barren of repast" is that "Augusta," Queen Elizabeth herself, "will restore, / The wrongs that learning beares of covetousnes / And Courts disdaine, the enemie to Arte" (Prol., 65–68). "Covetousness" and "disdain" are synonyms, in this context, for "envy," a word threaded through the poem itself, and each term applies equally to vilified art and political chicanery. Just as the poem honoring the Garter sees Elizabeth as a new Edward III restoring the Order, so, too, perhaps will come a new age of patronage, a restoration of learning.

By addressing Northumberland directly and naming contemporary poets and their misfortunes, Peele gives the poem a highly personal cast. This quality continues in the form—a dream-vision—he chooses to celebrate "The Honour of the Honourable Order of the Garter." Peele imagines a massive, almost eternal Garter procession, stretching from the Order's founding to the present day. As the dream-procession passes through the sky, making its way to Windsor Castle, seat of the Order of the Garter, Peele recalls the romantic anecdote of the garter's origin (lines 112–31). Later, "Fame" shows the dreamer "a golden Booke," a "Register . . . Consecrate to S. Georges chosen Knights" (173, 181–82). This register allows Peele to identify the famous knights who follow Edward III in the heavenly concourse; he lists them all, "the first / Created of that order by the King" (232–33). Even here, contemporary Elizabethan matters are not far away. In order to insinuate a comment on the Elizabethan earl of Southampton, Peele makes his ancestor (incorrectly)[30] one of the original Knights of the Garter (lines 210–18). As he did in describing the Accession Day tilts, Peele has understood completely the contemporary political value of revived medieval ceremony. Delight as they may in the spectacle, neither the poet nor the more thoughtful of his readers can miss the implied connections: Edward III and Elizabeth I; ancient loyalty and modern duty; ancestral heroism and contemporary courage. Placing a fictitious earl of Southampton among Edward's train is, in fact, the literary equivalent of dressing modern political issues in fancy armor or, more humbly, in the allegorical personifications of the Lord Mayor's pageant.

As witness and recorder, Peele can shape the poem to link the Order of the Garter with the status of poetry. Honor, fame, glorious accomplishment, *and* poetry suffer the same detraction: "Yet in the house of Fame and Courtes of Kings, / Envy will bite, or snarle and barke" (340–41). In Peele's imagination, Edward must assure his knights that their names will remain registered "Out of Oblivions reach, or Envies shot" (411). With the brief Epilogue, the strategy becomes clear. The poem compliments Northumberland and honors the Garter, but it redirects that honor toward the poet's social role and station:

> And then thought I: were it as once it was,
> But long agoe, when learning was in price,
> And Poesie with Princes gracious:
> I would adventure to set downe my dreame,
> In honour of these newe advaunced Lords
> S. Georges Knights. I was encouraged
> And did as I have doone. . . . (Epilogue, 2–8)

The Elizabethan revival of the Order of the Garter is unquestionably part of the period's politics as well as part of its hankering after romantic chivalry. Peele seized these facts as an opportunity to make poetry and political life parallel. Patronage *is* heroical. Just as a self-conscious and mildly *ersatz* medievalism may assist modern political propaganda (or truth, as Peele probably believed), so too the poet may employ the same tactic to restore a long-lost respect for his art.

Conclusion

In these courtly and civic poems, Peele is more than a hack journalist or Grub Street penny-a-word man. The earl of Northumberland's three pounds, or the money paid by the Salters' or Skinners' Company, were vital, no doubt. At the same time, Peele shared the social, religious, and political anxieties of his particularly anxious time, and these concerns appear again and again in his poems. Sometimes, as in *Anglorum Feriae,* they even seem to unbalance the poem; on the other occasions, as in *Descensus Astraeae,* the full design may have escaped its principal audience. Throughout all these poems, it is nonetheless possible to trace a professional poet's attempt to earn a living, to give value for money, and to express his culture's abiding interests. He certainly understood the way in which public ceremony has a social function, and he was no less adept when inventing fictions for the court, as *The Araygnement of Paris* and *The Old Wives Tale* show.

Chapter Three

A Second Troy: Elizabeth's England and *The Araygnement of Paris*

The Araygnement of Paris is "Peele's 'diploma piece,'" his first professional play, and comes from the period when he returned to London and set out to make a living as a writer.[1] Its narrative revolves around the origin of the Trojan War, a subject which fascinated the Elizabethans. The play calls England itself "a seconde Troie" because legendary history claimed that descendants of Priam's house had founded first Rome and later Britain. Peele had already written about Troy, probably while he was still at Oxford; his rather stilted poem, *A Tale of Troy,* appeared in 1589, but he said then that it was "an olde Poeme."[2] Although *The Araygnement of Paris* echoes several lines from the earlier poem, it is vastly more sophisticated, just the sort of thing an ambitious and bright young writer might hope to create as his first public effort. Peele combines legendary material (the Trojan War) with mythological beings (Venus, Pallas, Juno, and other Olympian gods and the so-called "Country Gods") and adds both to a pastoral setting (complete with names and a line lifted from Spenser's recently published *Shepherd's Calendar*) and a final compliment to Queen Elizabeth.[3] W. W. Greg thought Peele's skill in uniting this diverse material marked him "as pre-eminent among his contemporaries," but other critics have accused the play of disunity and confusion.[4]

The play's narrative moves from a prologue introducing Ate, goddess of discord, and the famous golden apple for which Venus, Pallas, and Juno will compete, to five short acts culminating with Queen Elizabeth's receiving the apple. The first act introduces the country gods, the three Olympian goddesses, and Paris's own love, the shepherdess Oenone. During a storm in the second act, Ate produces the golden apple of discord; the goddesses appeal to Paris, and he chooses Venus. Act 3 includes various scenes of hapless pastoral love affairs and the summons of Venus and Paris to an Olympian court of appeals. In Act 4, Paris defends himself, and the gods decide to let Diana make the final selection of the fairest goddess. The very brief final act shows Diana's choice of Queen Elizabeth, "This Paragon" (1166), as the fairest and concludes with a chorus sung by the three Fates, who resign their symbols to Elizabeth's control.

Literary and Dramatic Context

Despite its brevity (about 1,255 lines), *The Araygnement* includes many heterogeneous literary traditions, modes, conventions, and materials.[5] These matters need not, however, produce artistic chaos, especially when we consider the context of the play's performance and Peele's probable goals over and above the aesthetic. The play is a court entertainment, "Presented," as the title page states, "before the Queenes Majestie, by the Children of her Chappell." As such, it has many features which would not appear or would appear much less prominently in a play designed for the public stage or even for the private children's theater. Many qualities recall the court masque: for example, the emphasis on song, music, dance, and spectacle. Moreover, *The Araygnement* echoes, but does not quite reproduce, the masque's *sine qua non*—the final collapse of dramatic illusion, the breach of stage-audience distinctions in a concluding dance which unites the actors with selected members of their audience. While Peele's entertainment does not end with a dance, it does cross the boundary between impersonation and courtly environment when Diana awards the golden apple to a member of her audience, the queen.

The masque was a formal, prepared, and eventually very elaborate court spectacle intended for indoor presentation. Another less coherent genre of court revel also influenced *The Araygnement:* the outdoor entertainments which traditionally welcomed the queen to the noble homes she visited during her progresses. These entertainments, for example the most famous and costly one at Kenilworth Castle in 1575, or Sidney's *Lady of May* (Wanstead, 1578), or the one at Elvetham in 1591, also included symbolic personages and often employed both pastoral human characters and figures like Peele's country gods and Olympian deities.[6] *The Araygnement*'s opening scenes dramatize the persons and circumstances which Elizabeth often met on such occasions: sylvan deities, the countryside, pastoral pursuits. Thus, despite the subtitle, "A Pastorall," it is wrong to stress too exclusively the literary pastoral as an antecedent or source for *The Araygnement.* Very possibly, Peele seeks to re-create an ambience equally artificial but also more objectively present, that is, the physical circumstances of a progress and its celebrations.[7]

The play's subject matter and especially the mingled literary traditions and conventions recall many entertainments. The external form, however, appears rather different. Except at the very end, *The Araygnement* has a drama's separateness from its audience. Its narrative deploys more complicated relations (parallels and antitheses, for example) then do the progress entertainments, and its length and large cast of characters further distinguish it from them. If, however, we accept the implied similarities between the play's opening and the physical facts of an outdoor entertainment presented before the queen, it is not difficult to see other likenesses. The principal change between an elaborate entertainment and *The Araygnement* is the fact that the play comes to its chief spectator rather than vice versa. Were the play's material to be divided and presented at several different locations or even on several different days, to a queen "surprised" as she moved to or from the hunt or a firework display or some other sport, *The Araygnement* would resemble a progress-entertainment quite closely. Indeed, the different elements—the country gods, the pastoral love affairs, the Judgment of Paris—have numerous separate analogues among surviving progress-entertainments. What Peele has done is to accept a static viewer, the queen, and parade the entertainment before her instead of letting her come to its various segments *en passante.* This change alone forces the poet to invent an explanatory narrative which could give his diverse materials some rational order because he lacked the "frame" provided by the traveling monarch herself. Critics may complain that the plot does not weld its materials together, but Peele undertook an immense task in trying to convert the naive and basically anecdotal progress shows into a court play resembling John Lyly's sophisticated dramas.

Discord and Judgment

The title, the prologue, and the first act of *The Araygnement* all suggest that discord, argument, conflict, and their resolution are the organizing principles of the play and the fictive world it portrays. Although Peele uses the classical story of Paris's choice in very sophisticated ways, his title shows that he has shifted the emphasis toward the judging of Paris's judgment. The Trojan prince's choice itself, the pressures and desires and human alternatives it embodies, is less important than what follows that choice. Paris will be arraigned and with him all human history. Ate's famous blank-verse prologue offers two comprehensive motives for the following action.[8] Her first seventeen lines concern the "bane of Troie" (6); "the gods above" have decided that "Proude Troy must fall" (8), and Ate merely advances the divine behest. Alongside this moral explanation for Troy's fall, Ate mentions another:

> So loath and weerie of her heavie loade
> The Earth complaynes unto the hellish prince,
> Surcharged with the burden that she nill [will not] sustaine.
> Th'unpartiall daughters of Necessitie [the Fates]
> Bin aydes in her sute. . . . (17–21)

Some force in the nature of things—the Earth, the Fates—requires that warfare diminish the human race. Man's choice does not enter into this explanation; neither Troy's grandeur nor her pride sways impartial destruction. Ate ends her prologue with the conventional call for quiet and a final reminder of the future:

> . . . Lordinges adieu,
> Imposing silence for your taske, I ende,
> Till just assemblie of the goddesses
> Make me beginne the Tragedie of Troie. (26–29)

The tragedy of Troy will begin when the goddesses argue over the golden apple (lines 355ff.), but Peele first examines conflict among the "country gods" and their human subjects, the shepherds and shepherdesses of "Ida vales."

The first three scenes trace a series of arrivals and meetings among a group of rural deities gathering to greet and offer gifts to the Olympian deities. Conflict appears immediately. The gods argue over whose gift is the best and whether they have arrived too late. Pan finally must end the dispute: "Peace man for shame . . . we meete not now to brawle" (46–47). Pomona bustles in, sounding like any English citizen anxious to catch a glimpse of a queen, or a goddess, as she passes by. Her greatest worry, like that of her fellows, is the nature of her gift: "Thinkest Faunus that these goddesses will take our giftes in woorth" (55). He answers, as Duke Theseus does on a similar occasion in *A Midsummer Night's Dream,* that true gentleness accepts a gift as it is given and not for its intrinsic worth, "For gentlie takes the gentleman that oft the clowne [peasant] will scorne" (59). This exchange initiates a series of conversations and episodes devoted to gift-giving and gift-receiving, an extremely important variant of the discord/judgment structure Peele has given the play.[9] Most obviously, Peele has here incorporated a plea for his own offering. The play will end with a gift of itself and the golden apple to the queen. The last remaining rural goddess, Flora, arrives, and the figures on stage unite in various acts of harmonious welcome: *"An artificiall charme of birdes"* carols a greeting, the country gods respond antiphonally, and then they dance "a hornepype all gallant in glee" (178). At last the Olympian goddesses enter and, as predicted, graciously acknowledge the welcome: "these signes of your goodwill / Wee take in worth, and shall accept them still" (224–25).

Human Conflict. This opening movement of discord harmonized into welcome and contentment ends with the appearance of the play's first human characters, Paris and his love, Oenone. They, too, seem at peace. Oenone has a "sweete alluring face," and Paris is her "hartes contentment" (238, 242). As true inhabitants of Renaissance pastoral, Paris and Oenone proceed to storytelling and the singing of a song. Paris asks her to tell a story which he will accompany on his "pype." When she reviews her repertoire (carefully numbered in the margin), her tales prove to be catastrophic ones, largely drawn from Ovid's *Metamorphoses.* They concern "love offence" (265: Pluto and Prosperpina) or "how forme [beauty] doth vade [fade]" (269: Narcissus) or "what force in love, what wit in sorrow dwelles" (271: Philomela). Like Hermia's description of how "the course of true love never did run smooth" in *A Midsummer Night's Dream,* this list promises future unhappiness despite present pleasure. Paris and Oenone decide to sing "Cupids curse," one of the most beautiful of Renaissance English lyrics, with the chorus, "They that do chaunge olde love for new, pray gods they chaunge for worse" (283). Paris claims that "our musicke" will symbolize "the love that growes twixt thee and me" (287), but of course it only anticipates the moment when Paris will earn Cupid's curse, for he will soon abandon Oenone and gain the much more destructive love of Helen. Paris concludes the song by affirming his vow, carved upon what Oenone calls "our Poplar tree" (285): "My vowe is made and witnessed, the Poplar will not starte, / Nor shall the nymphe Oenones love from forth my breathing hart" (316–17). Peele's irony is strong, because the poplar was a conventional symbol of *in*constancy, as it had been in the Kenilworth entertainment of 1575, to which *The Araygnement* often seems to allude.[10]

Although Peele later introduces other shepherds and their lives to serve as parallels with Paris and Oenone, the first act has largely presented the ingredients for the play's conflicts and, very subtly, their resolution. He has sketched the landscape, conventionally pastoral in contents and beauty, but also possessing the allegorical qualities which pastoral traditionally invites. Flora's praise of her handiwork is unusual only in the graceful verse Peele employs:

> Not Iris in her pride and braverie,
> Adornes her arche with such varietie:
> Nor doth the milke white way in frostie night,
> Appeare so faire and beautifull in sight:
> As done these fieldes, and groves, and sweetest bowres,
> Bestrewed and deckt with partie collord flowers.
> Alonge the bubling brookes and silver glyde,
> That at the bottome doth in sylence slyde,
> The waterie flowers and lillies on the bankes,
> Like blazing cometes burgen all in rankes:
> Under the Hathorne and the Poplar tree,
> Where sacred Phoebe may delight to be:
> The Primerose and the purple Hyacinthe,
> The dayntie Violet and the holsome Minthe:
> The dooble Daisie, and the Couslip queene
> Of sommer floures, do over peere the greene. . . . (78–93)

The Revels office seems to have provided some elaborate stage decor, because Flora's tribute proves to be symbolic representations of the goddesses worked in flowers (102–35). Flora concludes that Venus "for her wreath of roses" (the stage decoration itself) will not dare "With Floras cunning counterfet compare" (124–25) and she concludes, self-consciously,

> So that what lyving whight [being] shall chaunce to see,
> These goddesses, eche placed in her degree,

> Portrayed by Floraes workemanshipe alone,
> Must say that Arte and nature met in one. (126–29)

The lines half-acknowledge the court audience ("lyving whight") and ask their approval for the elaborate scenic decor, but they also emphasize the artificiality of the literary and dramatic "place" the goddess inhabits. Through emblematic or realistic staging, Juno, Pallas, and Venus become the landscape of *The Araygnement.* They and their competing qualities constitute the world of Mount Ida, although we also know that Diana is "mistresse of our woodes" (50) just as Diana's earthly avatar, Queen Elizabeth, is mistress of England. Artifice, in both stage machinery and divine deceit, will return when the goddesses require Paris to choose among them.

Divine Conflict. Venus and Juno substantiate Oenone's forboding list of stories when they enter, *"ex abrupto,"* arguing about the love affairs and peccadilloes of Jupiter and other deities (320ff.). Pallas tries to calm the discord: "No more of this, fayre goddesses, unrip not so your shames, / To stand all naked to the world, that bene such heavenly dames" (346–47). At the moment, of course, the heavenly dames appear no less fickle, jealous, and spiteful than the "tatling trull" Juno calls the nymph Echo, or than Thestilis, the human shepherdess who jilts the shepherd Corin in Act 3. Their quarreling appropriately cues the sudden storm (*"of thunder and lightning"* says the stage direction) which allows Ate to "trundle" the golden ball on stage. Like many Renaissance emblems and like the devices which greeted Elizabeth on ceremonial entries or in the Tiltyard on 17 November, the golden ball has a motto (or "breyfe"), *"Detur Pulcherrimae,"* and a "poesie," "Let this unto the fayrest gyven be" (367).[11] True to their natures, the goddesses immediately dispute possession of the apple. Juno claims it for "majestye" (371), Venus because "The name of Venus is in deede but beautye" (379), and Pallas demands the award for "beautye of the minde" (388). As Venus admits, the problem is one of interpretation: "Wee must not conster heereof as yow meane" (400), and Pallas diagnoses a general stubbornness: "heres none mee thinkes disposed to yeelde" (405). They resolve to accept chance; the next passer-by "must be umpier in this controversie" (416).

That umpire is Paris, of course, and with his arrival the divine and human intersect for the first time. Discord has allowed chance to enter the supernatural realm, and with chance comes human error: "Sheepeherd, abash not, though, at sudden thus, / Thou be aryved by ignorance among us" (423–24). In fact, the goddesses are no less ignorant than Paris. No more than he do they understand where the golden apple comes from, or the significance of their decision and his. Their envious ambition urges them to compete, heedless of the consequences and willing to accept an arbitrary judge and judgment. As each goddess makes her plea to Paris, Peele deploys the extravagant spectacle which links *The Araygnement* with masques and other court entertainments. Juno produces *"a Tree of gold laden with Diadems and Crownes of golde";* Pallas offers "wysdomes worthines" (467) and the "honor of chyvallrye" (469) in a dance of nine armored knights.[12] Venus wins the contest by conjuring Helen *"in her braverie,"* and this "lasse of Venus court" (494) sings an Italian song describing the chaste Diana as a goddess presiding over unhappy and doomed love affairs. Forced, but also eager, to make a decision, Paris chooses Venus, "Whose sweetenes dothe bothe gods and creatours move" (524). After Venus has taken Paris off to his reward, Juno vows revenge: "heaven and earth just witnesses shall bee, / I will revenge it on his progenye" (533–34).

The choices Paris faces had long been allegorized as alternative lives—contemplation, civic action, sensuality, for example—and Peele alludes to the traditional interpretations. He also comments more subtly on pastoralism itself, when Juno first recalls that "olde shepherds [that is, poets] title workes of fame" to her and then offers a rather terrifying glimpse of pastoral artificiality:

> The moulde whereon thowe treadest shall be of Tagus sandes,
> And Xanthus shall runne liquid golde for the to wash thy handes:
> And yf thou lyke to tend thy flock, and not from them to flie,
> Their fleeces shalbe curled gold to please their masters eye. (451–54)

Typical gold-and-enamel pastoral similes here become a Midas-world of gold sheep, gold water, gold earth. Her promises make Flora's claim—"Arte and nature met in one"—into a nightmarish vision where divinity overwhelms nature rather than supporting and vivifying it. Nor is Pallas's union of wisdom and war much more comforting. Paris may simultaneously "fly above, / Ycrowned with fame neere to the seate of Jove" (465–66) and "bee renouned for happy victorie, / To fighte it out" (470–71). The shows are indices of the Elizabethan understanding of pastoral as both a synthesis and an analysis of all human affairs. Finally, Helen's extraordinary song challenges the very goddess of the pastoral world. Diana, "mistresse of our woodes" and hostess of the visiting Olympian goddesses (192–213), has yet to appear in the play, but Helen attacks her in Venus's name. The song's first three stanzas ennumerate Diana's attributes, and the last stanza overthrows them:

> Io son un Diana dolce e rara
> Che con Le guardi Io posso far guerra
> A Dian' in fern' in cielo, et in terra (506–8)
>
> (I am [a] Diana gentle and rare
> for with my glances I can make war
> on Diana in hell, in heaven, and on earth)[13]

The moral consequences of Paris's choice are nothing less than the inversion of the pastoral world, and again, the pastoral fiction allows Peele to comment on the "historical" consequences: the Trojan War. It will be the work of the latter part of *The Araygnement* to restore Diana and, with her, both the natural world and Troy.

After Paris's choice, and with Juno's threat still echoing, Peele introduces the remaining human characters. They have Spenserian pastoral names—Colin, Hobinol, Digon, Thenot, Thestilis—and they are all involved in seeking or denying love or lamenting its effects. In part, Peele may only be filling in the pastoral background and padding out his short play, but the juxtaposition of Colin's lament (537–52) and the chorus of shepherds who comment on the paradoxical emotion which "gives us bane to bring us lowe, and let us medicine lacke" (556) with the scene in which Paris chooses Venus strongly implies that we are watching both the unexamined context and the consequence of that choice. Thenot rightly, if rather grouchily, observes that Love is no friend to sheep, "For sure this love doth nothing else but make our herdmen weepe" (560). No sooner has Colin departed (to die, as we soon learn), than Oenone enters to complete the parallel: "False *Paris,* this was not thy vow, when thou and I were one, / To raung and chaung old love for new: but now those dayes be gone" (585–86). The echo of their earlier duet promises that Paris will suffer "Cupids curse." As Oenone sings her "Complaint" (good enough to be anthologized in *Englands Helicon*) and strips her poplar wreath, Mercury enters in pursuit of Paris.

Peele now exploits the pastoral plot in what might be called "the arraignment of Thestilis," an anticipation of Paris's own. Mercury tells Oenone that he comes

> To cease [seize] upon the man whom thou dost love,
> To summon him before my father Jove,
> To answere matter of great consequence,
> And Jove himselfe will not be longe from hence. (646–49)

Before the "messenger of Heaven" finds the culprit, however, Venus herself becomes a judge in the case of Colin (now dead) and Thestilis, the shepherdess who spurned him. She assures the plaintiffs, Colin's fellow shepherds, that she will take "A straunge revenge upon the maide and her disdaine" (669). This severe judgment disturbs Paris, because he, too, is similarly guilty: "But tell me, gracious goddesse, for a starte and false offence, / Hath Venus or her sonne the power, at pleasure to dispence" (682–83). When Venus describes the torments of disdainful and faithless lovers, Paris begins to recognize the power he so glibly invoked when awarding Venus the apple. She does indeed "bothe gods and creatours move" (524). The goddess admonishes him:

> Be true and stedfast in thy love, beware thou doe disguise thee.
> For he that makes but love a jest, when pleaseth him to starte,
> Shall feele those firye water drops [in Hell] consume
> his faithles harte. (693–95)

A dumb show, recalling the shows the goddesses used to woo Paris, reveals Thestilis vainly pursuing *"a foule croked Churle"* who *"crabedly refuzeth her."*

Paris's Trial. Scenes of judgment and the analysis of vows and laws have filled the play as a prelude to Paris's arraignment. Peele delays the trial long enough to show us the double standard that governs Olympian and human love affairs. As Vulcan eagerly pursues one of Diana's nymphs, he and Bacchus argue about divine immorality. Vulcan's defense—"Why may not Vulcan treade awry, aswell as Venus dooth?" (795)—mocks his wife's high-minded judgments in the preceding scene. The nymph answers the gods' bawdy as nimbly as she escapes their pursuit, and Bacchus contents himself with insult: "A peevish elvish shroe" (814). The phrase boomerangs, however, when Neptune immediately complains about Venus: "It is a worke of wit and toyle to rule a lustie shroe" (821). Here again Peele has reworked ordinary pastoral matter (heavy-handed Olympian humor, Bacchic revelry, the plight of Diana's nymph) to explore the play's "legal" and amorous issues. Different laws control human and divine actions. Venus takes up Paris, "my lovely boy" (692), for her own purposes, but she cannot change either her own laws—stringently applied to Thestilis—or the dictates of Olympus. While the goddesses have human failings, it is the pastoral characters who suffer the consequences. Venus may bluster,

> Let Juno jet, and Pallas play her parte,
> What heere I have, I woonne it by deserte:
> And heaven and earthe shall bothe confounded bee,
> Ere wronge in this be donne to him or me (771–74),

but Mercury is right: "This litle fruite, yf Mercury can spell [decipher, predict], / Will sende I feare a world of soules to hell" (775–76).

At last, when the pantheon has gathered in "Dianaes bower" and Paris has been "araygned of parciallitie, / Of sentence partiall and unjust" (848–49), Paris begins his defense. His speeches are superb, and Peele (or the printer) clearly thought them a selling point because the quarto has an indented subheading, *"Paris oration to the Councell of the gods."*[14] Paris develops his defense in the manner recommended by classical rhetoricians and taught to Elizabethan schoolchildren. First, he compliments the court (853–62), offers self-deprecation, and promises to be brief (863–67). He admits the deed, but excuses it on four grounds: he was commanded to judge; he is only human; if he made an error, it was an error of physical and psychological weakness (his eyesight), not premeditation or intent; finally, others—the gods themselves—would have made the same choice (868–81). Having made these concessions and offered extenuating arguments, Paris now attacks the charge of partiality. That charge has no force, he claims, since he had never met the goddesses before. Once again, he returns to a most important issue: the choice "was referd from them to me" (893). Asked to judge, he judged. Paris is obviously making a good impression: both Pluto and Neptune compliment his argumentative skills (886, 897–98).

Paris has blamed his "dazled eye" (873 and 896), but he can "adde reason for my deede" (899). Like the other goddesses, Venus has one special quality. Since beauty and not "majestie" (Juno) or "wisedome" (Pallas) was in question, Venus won the contest. Paris now explains his credentials. He has "learnd to ken the fayrest of the flocke" (916) and, an important qualification, he judges "but by natures ayme" (917). Once more he returns to the central inequity: he was a "dayesman," or mediator, "chosen there by full consent, / And heavenly powers should not repent their deedes" (919–20). As any good lawyer would, Paris now admits the contrary hypothesis: suppose he did judge corruptly? This portion of the speech (925–43) is very tricky indeed, but Paris returns again to his ability to judge only beauty, "The thing that hath enchaunted heaven it selfe" (933). Moreover, a shepherd has no need of wealth or arms, the gifts Pallas and Juno could command. Corrupt or not, Paris claims he would make the same decision. Paris ends his oration with a plea and final justification: his soul is "guiltles," his thought "faultles." Once more, Paris arraigns the court. If his choice is to be reversed "by appeale," then "The wronge, the hurte not mine, if anie be, / But hers whose beautie claymed the prize of me" (950–51).

This speech deserves detailed study because it reveals a great deal about the first four acts and completes Peele's design for the play's resolution. Above all, the speech is effective. Jupiter admits, "if you will but justice in the cause, / The man must quited be by heavens lawes" (956–57). Again and again, Paris has claimed that he was placed in a double bind: forced to decide, he could not help but offend. Further, his status—a human shepherd—made the choice inevitable. As pastoral man, he is free of economic or political ambition; thus he claims to act "by natures ayme" which includes both a "dazled eye" and "reason." Paris may be trapped by nature and divine command, but Peele has also managed to uncover some inconsistencies lurking within the Elizabethan poetic pastoral. To attack Paris's choice, either in literal or allegorical terms, is to challenge the genre itself, or at least some of the sophisticated fantasies it embodies. The catastrophic war which all the gods acknowledge must follow this event makes Peele's exploration of the pastoral as tense and thoughtful as the parallel exploration in Shakespeare's romantic comedies.

Resolution. Although Paris has defended himself successfully, he must fulfill his allotted destiny: "His payne, his payne, his never dying payne, / A cause to make a many moe complaine" (980–81). Jupiter dismisses him: "Goe take thy way to Troie, and there abide thy fate" (985). The original problem still remains, and Peele's very human presentation of the gods solves it elegantly. Having agreed to retry the issue, the gods find they can reach no more satisfactory conclusion than Paris did. Apollo, complaining that "womens witts woorke mens unceasinge woes" (1042), introduces a new "holly Lawe of heaven" (1051). "One god" cannot "medle in an others powre" (1052), so Diana is "the fittest judge" because the crisis occurred "so neere" her "bowre" and "in her owne territorie" (1053, 1055, 1061). The male gods eagerly embrace this piece of "sacred wit" since it frees "the blame from us and trouble cleane" (1071, 1072).

The final act is a single long scene revealing Diana's decision. True to the legalistic atmosphere, she first requires that the contesting goddesses swear to accept her judgment. Each goddess vows agreement, concluding with a formula: Pallas, Juno, and Venus "shall rest content and satisfied, / And say the best desert doth there [in whomever Diana selects] abide" (1106–7, 1118–19, and 1136–37). The stage directions now helpfully explain: *"Diana having taken their othes speaketh. Diana describeth the Nymphe Eliza a figure of the Queene."* Diana describes Eliza and Elizium, "A kingdome that may well compare with mine. / An auncient seat of kinges, a seconde Troie" (1152–53). This Eliza, or "Zabeta," as Pallas calls her, is a "Paragon . . . In whom do meete so manie giftes" (1166–67) that she incorporates the best qualities of Juno, Pallas, Venus, and Diana herself. All the goddesses immediately accept that to Eliza "this ball in merit doth belonge" (1175) and agree to join Diana at an annual ceremony at which "the dames of life and destinie" (the three Fates) "repayre, / To this renowned Queene so wise and fayre, / With pleasaunt songes this peereles nimphe to greete" (1198–1200).

The Play and the Queen

Clotho, Lachesis, and Atropos promptly appear and sing a Latin song. A stage direction urges, *"The state being in place,"* that is, Queen Elizabeth being enthroned to watch the play. Each Fate resigns the symbol of her office (distaff, reel, and knife) to the queen and prays, as Atropos says, "Live longe the noble Phoenix of our age, / Our fayre Eliza our Zabeta fayre" (1235–36).[15] This "rare solemnitie" is an extraordinary scene. Queen Elizabeth controls the most fearsome and inexplicable energies the Elizabethan mind could imagine. Diana twice says the event is "far contrarie kinde . . . A favour far in deed contrarie kinde" (1204, 1239). What we see does violate "kinde," or nature, because this Phoenix, this Paragon, may weave "her web of life" as best suits her. Elizabeth now receives the golden apple as a token of Olympian approval, and the characters sing an epilogue (in Latin) praising Elizabeth's chastity, purity, and learning.[16] The play itself thus becomes a final gift and tribute, joining the Fates' terrible implements and the much-disputed golden apple.

As *Polyhymnia* and *Anglorum Feriae* demonstrate, the Accession Day tilts were above all contests in honor of the queen. Her chivalric status enforced the tournaments and her implicit or explicit approval endorsed the winners, who naturally claimed that she subsumed their honor, abilities, and accomplishments. Similarly, the Lord Mayor's pageants elaborately acknowledge Elizabeth's presiding authority and her importance to London's happiness and even the city's very existence. In outline, these patterns duplicate the goddesses' submission to Elizabeth at the end of *The Araygnement.* Equally, the pattern appears in the country-house revels which always include contests to honor the queen. When Elizabeth arrived at Kenilworth Castle, for example, she received the country gods' finest gifts, and George Gascoigne's unperformed play for that occasion makes the queen the embodiment of Venus and Diana. Years later, in the Mitchum entertainment (12–13 September 1598), we find again "a 'contention' or dispute . . . between two or more speakers vying for supremacy in honoring the Queen."[17] The structure also appears in *The Lady of May,* the Theobalds entertainment (May 1591), and a very late entertainment given by Robert Cecil in London (December 1602).[18]

Such courtly devices—tilts, masques, country-house revels, or court plays—almost always have a persuasive or didactic element. They are anchored in the moment and the situation: in 1613, George Chapman wrote of his own masque that "all these courtly, and honouring inventions . . . should expressively-arise out of the places, and persons for and by whome they are presented. . . ."[19] Inevitably, they urge some action or reaction upon their chief spectator.

The desired response might be very specific, as in *The Lady of May* or Essex's show in the 1595 tilt, or it could be rather general, the maintenance of good government or true religion.[20] The implication for *The Araygnement* is that the play is not just flattery or a praise of Elizabeth's power to harmonize discord or a celebration of her place as a monarch whose "New Troy" restores the ruined towers of Ilium or even an effort to describe her semidivine power to recall the Golden Age.[21] The reciprocity of an idealized world (here the pastoral song-dance-drama) with courtly reality also works in the other direction. Elizabeth witnesses *The Araygnement* and learns or reaffirms the need for conciliation in the England of the early 1580s. The play illustrates political discord. Accepting the golden apple, Elizabeth also accepts responsibility for ending discord. She notes love's divisive, painful, and far-reaching effects—up to the gods themselves, forward and backward in human history. From Venus's attack on Diana (in Helen's song) to Diana's status as Olympian judge to her submission before Elizabeth, we watch an ascending series of authorities. *The Araygnement* takes place in a landscape which is first that of the three competing goddesses, then Diana's "territorie," and lastly Elizabeth's England, "A kingdome," as Diana says, "that may well compare with mine." Love must be ruled. If, as M. C. Bradbrook rightly claims, "Envy was to the Poet what Danger was to the courtly lover" and if "during the reign of Envy . . . the commonwealth falls into decay," we can recognize a further link between the lover's happiness or unhappiness and the state's condition.[22] Ultimately the symbolic interchange between court and courtly entertainment, a symbol made literal when Elizabeth intervenes, makes *The Araygnement* a social and political, as well as a literary and dramatic, event.

A repeated motif of courtly revel and country-house pageant is the honored spectator's power to produce harmony. We have seen an overt form in Elizabeth's role as judge among competing ways of life or competing devotees. A more obscure but equally common harmonizing power is one that draws a social maverick, an outcast, or isolated figure (e.g., the wild man, the hermit, or the pilgrim) into a social concord, into "civility." One may describe this act as "liberation," but its usual image is some form of incorporation or acceptance.[23] This fiction extends back to Henry VIII's court entertainments.[24] In his daughter's case, the fiction usually emphasizes her interlocutors' helpless and often grateful inability to resist adoring her. Loyalty enforces society. Individual, asocial, and even antisocial desires collapse into allegiance. That is, the fictions manifest the very pattern the court revels themselves sought to impose upon the world at large.

The Bisham entertainment of 1592 describes the queen "leading affections in fetters."[25] *The Araygnement of Paris* develops this pattern extensively. The queen triumphs over lust for station or for other human and divine women, and she goes on to dominate history and even those powers—fate, destiny, necessity—which control the gods themselves. Thus, practical security (the rule of law, justice, monarchy) and metaphysical stability (the defeat of Troy's enemies, of the envious gods, of time) require Elizabeth's existence. Peele diagrams not merely the flow of domination and the ebbing return of loyalty, he adds Diana-Elizabeth's very control over nature itself. Without her, society would fragment. Worse, men would fall prey to incalculable cosmic power: capricious, unjust, passionate.

Recovering the context of courtly revel allows us to form a less "intrinsic" judgment of *The Araygnement:* we can better appreciate the play's underlying political and even personal motives (and motifs) and better assess Peele's accomplishment. Court entertainments provide a different measure of artistic success from that implied when we compare *The Araygnement* either with Lyly's more discretely dramatized efforts or with later dramatic tradition. At the same time, we can recognize that *The Araygnement*'s remarkable synthesis—of mythology, pastoral, and politics, for instance—unifies not only, perhaps not even primarily, learned and literary traditions, but rather serves as an early and artistically persuasive fusion of various aristocratic preoccupations.

Chapter Four

Things That Seem Are Not the Same: *The Old Wives Tale*

In all of Peele's varied productions, none is so mysterious as *The Old Wives Tale,* published in 1595. Although the title page claims it was "played by the Queenes Majesties players," no contemporary record of a performance exists. In style, subject matter, construction, and even in its very short length, the play seems to be utterly *sui generis*. This absence of any historical or dramatic context has made the play very difficult to interpret. Although the play's events derive almost entirely from age-old folklore sources, Peele seems to have used few, if any, of the recorded Elizabethan versions of those stories.[1] These simple stories and their romantic trappings are presented within a remarkable "frame," formed by a pair of characters, Frolicke and Fantasticke, who listen to a third character, Madge, while she tells "an old wives winters tale" (96). No sooner has she begun a rather stumbling introduction than the characters of her story enter and perform the tale she has started to narrate. Madge, Frolicke, and Fantasticke remain on stage throughout the play and occasionally comment on the action, although the other characters never address them. Once the play or tale has ended, we return to Madge's cottage and to her two listeners, who thank her for the entertainment and, presumably, depart.

While this frame-structure has probably aroused the most interest in the play, it is also true that Peele manages to create an exceedingly complex linkage of simple stories within that frame. Even the barest account of the play's action requires painstaking effort, although virtually every episode is worked out at least to some degree. The frame and its complicated contents go a long way toward refuting the common charge that Peele's sense of dramatic construction was inferior to his verbal or poetic abilities. Some textual confusion leaves a few loose ends, but it is hard to believe that any audience could notice them in the theater. Certainly, the play's magical elements and its long-ago-and-far-away folkloric qualities disguise any logical or mathematical flaws in its construction. Moreover, magic and folklore combine with the exceedingly sophisticated frame-story to conceal Peele's connection with the play, that is, to hide the dramatist or any other "source" from our view.

The Action

In good romantic fashion, the play opens with three pages lost at night in a dark wood. They have been separated from their "yong master" (12), who has in any case devoted all his attention to "the faire Lady . . . the only Saint that he hath sworne to serve" (12–13).[2] The three pages, Anticke, Frolicke, and Fantasticke, are rescued by Clunch the blacksmith, who has been walking in the woods with "Ball my Dogge" (53); Clunch takes the strangers home to his wife, Madge, who offers them shelter and food. Now that they are safe, the boys prefer entertainment and sing a song, "When as the Rie reach to the chin." Then Anticke demands "a merry winters tale," and Fantasticke agrees that "a tale of an howre long were as good as an howres sleepe" (83, 85–86). Madge sends Clunch and Anticke off to bed and proceeds to ramble through the introduction of her tale. It begins very vaguely: "Once uppon a time there was a King or a Lord, or a Duke that had a faire daughter" (110–11). The daughter of course is "the fairest that ever was; as white as snowe, and as redd as bloud" (111–12). As is the fate of all fair princesses in folk tales, this one is stolen away, and her father dispatches all the young men in his kingdom to bring her back.

Madge's listeners, the pages Frolicke and Fantasticke, play the rational audience and ask, "Who drest [prepared] his [the king's] dinner then?" (116) and receive a bawdy answer: "either heare my tale, or kisse my taile" (117). Madge suddenly remembers that her story includes a conjurer, who "carried the Kinges Daughter away in his mouth to a Castle that hee made of stone" (121–22). Eventually, there are no rescuers left except the princess's two brothers, who duly set off to find their sister. Madge then interrupts her own story: "O I forget: she (he I would say) turned a proper yong man to a Beare in the night, and a man in the day, and keeps by a crosse that parts three severall waies, and he made his Lady run mad: gods me bones, who comes here?" (125–28). "Who comes here" are in fact the two brothers she has just been describing, and Frolicke understands immediately: "Soft Gammer, here some come to tell your tale for you" (129–30). The play now shifts into a dramatization of Madge's tale, but she and the two pages remain present throughout the rest of the entertainment, offering commentary and explanation from time to time.

The two brothers declare that they have arrived "Upon these chalkie Cliffs of Albion . . . to seeke faire Delya forth" (132, 135), and they soon meet another character Madge had mentioned, the old man who "keeps by a crosse." The brothers pity him, and each gives him an "Almes pennie." In response, the old man abruptly asks, "Was shee fayre?" (154). Since only one "she" has been mentioned so far, we know that the old man means the princess Delya, and her brothers have no doubt either, for one replies: "I [Aye], the fairest for white, and the purest for redd" (155), almost precisely the formula Madge had used. The old man then makes a prophecy—"my old spell"—that the brothers will get their wishes if they

> Be not afraid of every stranger,
> Start not aside at every danger:
> Things that seeme are not the same,
> Blow a blast at every flame. . . . (158–61)

This spell is promising and mysterious enough so that one brother repeats it, along with the old man's self-identification: "If any aske who told you this good, / Say the white Beare of Englands wood" (164–65 and 173–74).

After the brothers have left on their quest, the old man unselfconsciously tells the audience his "heavy tale" (177): "Sacrapant that cursed sorcerer" (185) has stolen the old man's "deerest love, my true betrothed wife" (187) and "worse than this . . . Did turne me straight unto an ugly Beare" (189–90). Now we understand the references to the "white Beare of Englands wood" and learn that the "old man" is in fact a young one suffering from Sacrapant's enchantment. Much later, we also learn that the "old man" is named "Erestus" (873). We might mistakenly think that the "deerest love" had something to do with Delya, so Peele immediately produces another woman, and the "Beare" (or old man, or young man) explains: "See where Venelya my betrothed love, / Runs madding all inrag'd about the woods" (197–98). It is also worth noticing that Venelia's appearance responds to the old man's story in much the same way that the two brothers had appeared in response to Madge's story.

The next episode concerns "Lampriscus my discontented neighbour" (200), who visits the old man to ask for advice on how to handle his two daughters, one beautiful but proud and shrewish, the other so ugly that no dowry could possibly encourage a husband to marry her. (In good folklore fashion, this daughter should be sweet-tempered, and so she proves later in the play.) Erestus advises his neighbor to send his daughters "to the Well for the water of life: there shall they finde their fortunes unlooked for [unexpectedly]" (238–39). Lampriscus and the old man now leave the stage, and Frolicke interrupts the play to ask Madge "was this the man that was a Beare in the night, and a man in the day?" She agrees that the man at the cross and the bear are one and the same, but suddenly notices some other figures approaching: "But soft, who comes here? O these are the harvest men; ten to one they sing a song of mowing" (247–49). The Harvesters (four would be a traditional number, although the text doesn't specify) then sing a song of sowing and leave the stage. Although they appear once again, the Harvesters are never clearly integrated into the plot.

Two new characters now appear, one with a two-handed sword and the other called "Booby the Clowne." Madge tells Fantasticke that these men are "going to the conjurer," and the man with the two-handed sword bombastically identifies himself as "Huanebango," who has "abandoned the Court and honourable company, to doo my devoyre [devoir, duty] against this sore Sorcerer and mighty Magitian" (271, 278–80). Huanebango and Booby are two more of the questers seeking Princess Delya. As they are about to continue their trip, the old man enters (or they come upon him at his cross). Huanebango refuses the old man alms, but Booby is kind to him and offers a piece of cake which he has refused to give Huanebango because he is so boastful. In return, the old man offers another prophecy, as he had to Delya's two brothers:

> He [Huanebango] shall be deafe when thou shalt not see;
> Farewell my sonne things may so hit,
> Thou maist have wealth to mend thy wit. (330–32)

These characters leave the stage, and a new figure appears and identifies himself as "Wretched and miserable Sacrapant" (339), although his conjurer's costume probably made him immediately identifiable. Sacrapant is "wretched" because while he has made himself appear "yong and pleasant," he is really "aged, crooked, weake and numbe" (348–49). Moreover, it appears that even though he has Delya under his spell, she has yet to "revive" him, that is, give in to his lustful demands. Delya appears and Sacrapant offers her anything she wants. She asks for the "best meate from the king of Englands table" and the "best wine in all France," all served "by the veriest knave in all Spaine" (362–64). Sacrapant complies, and the "veriest knave" proves to be a friar. Delya's brothers suddenly appear, and Sacrapant hustles her off the stage. Recalling the old man's encouraging prophecy, the two brothers draw their swords and start after Sacrapant, but the conjurer returns with lightning and thunder, enchants the brothers, and has them carried off by two furies. Sacrapant then explains to the audience that ordinary human strength cannot defeat his powers because there is a little flame burning in a glass hidden within a hill. Until "this fade," he says, "my skill shall still endure" (427). Sacrapant expects immortality for two oracular reasons: first, "never none shall breake this little glasse, / But she that's neither wife, widow, nor maide," and second, "this is thy destinie, / Never to die, but by a dead mans hand" (428–31). These magical promises are, of course, made to be broken in some unexpected and wonderful fashion, and so the play will show.

The play returns us once more to the old man at the cross and a new character whom the stage direction calls *"Eumenides the wandring Knight."* Like the two brothers, this knight also seeks Delya, and he too gets a mysterious promise from the old man:

> Bestowe thy almes, give more than all,
> Till dead mens bones come at thy call:
> Farewell my sonne, dreame of no rest,
> Til thou repent that thou didst best. (445–48)

After the old man leaves, four rustic characters enter, arguing over the burial fees for a dead man, "Jack, the frollickst frannion [gallant]" they ever knew (469–70). The Sexton and Churchwarden will not bury Jack until they are paid, and Jack's friends have no money. Eumenides offers almost all he has to pay the sum (only three halfpence are left), and he recalls Erestus's words: "Bestowe all thou hast, and this is all, / Till dead mens bones comes at thy call" (518–19). Madge and the pages now interrupt, and Madge tells them that Jack was "a marvelous fellow . . . a poore man, but very well beloved: you shall see anon what this Jack will come to" (530–32). The Harvesters enter again, and this time they appropriately sing a song of reaping (535–38).

Huanebango and his companion (now strangely called "Corebus") have made their way to Sacrapant's lair, and the magician performs some more crowd-pleasing magic ("*A voice and flame of fire,*" says the stage direction). He strikes down Huanebango, apparently making him deaf, and blinds his companion. Sacrapant now turns to the earlier threat, the two brothers, and reinforces his spell over Delya. The text is slightly confusing, but apparently the conjurer wants to make sure that Delya will not recognize her brothers (whom she must force to dig in the earth). Sacrapant renames Delya "Berecynthia" to indicate that "never shall she know hir selfe againe, / Untill that Sacrapant hath breathd his last" (572–73). Once again, an action in the play has incorporated into it the conclusion or reversal of that action. This pattern appears again and again, most obviously in the prophetic replies the old man gives when he receives alms. Delya dutifully and cruelly orders her brothers to dig, but they uncover the little light in the hill, which she orders them to "touch . . . not, it is some thing, / That my Lord hath hidden there" (605–6). Although the plot has by now grown exceedinglv complicated—and will soon become even more confusing—Peele constantly reminds us of important points (like the light under the hill) and uses prophecies and spells to promise us that all the divergent strands will be woven together.

Lampriscus's two daughters—Zantippa, the proud and pretty one, and Celanta, the ugly, sweet one—now appear with pitchers at the "well," just as the old man had advised. Zantippa curses her sister and breaks both pitchers. While they are offstage (presumably to fetch new pitchers), two furies put the dazed Huanebango down beside the well. Zantippa returns, and when she dips her pitcher into the well, a magic "Head" appears with this rhythmical promise:

> Gently dip, but not too deepe,
> For feare you make the golden beard to weepe,

> Faire maiden white and red,
> Stroke me smoothe, and combe my head,
> And thou shalt have some cockell bread. (635–39)

("Cockell bread" is a folk-custom bread supposed to win a woman a husband.)[3] Zantippa is characteristically shrewish and hits the head with her pitcher. Thunder and lightning awaken Huanebango, who is deaf, and he immediately starts to court the beautiful Zantippa. She curses him repeatedly, but of course he cannot hear and assumes that she is overcome with his fine speech (including some dreadful hexameters which he decides must be too complicated for her and foregoes in favor of prose). Zantippa sees that Huanebango will make a usefully indulgent husband and accepts him: "Lobb [bumpkin] be your comfort, and Cuckold bee your destenie . . . if you will have us, you had best say so betime" (682–84).

Eumenides now enters, quite forlorn since he has given away all his money and seems no nearer his goal. He is joined by a character who describes himself as "a neate handsome and cleanly yong Lad, about the age of fifteene or sixteene yeares" (700–701) and offers to become his companion and servant. This newcomer seems to be "a spirit" because he knows without asking that Eumenides is "the man . . . that came from a strange place in the land of Catita . . . to seeke out a Ladie as white as snowe, and as redd as blood . . ." (709–13). Although most of the women in the play are described in terms of "red" and "white," the colors of folklore as well as of Petrarchan love poetry, the audience will remember that these phrases and comparisons are precisely the ones Madge used when she first mentioned Delya (111–12 and cf. 155). Eumenides is astounded, but agrees to follow this new friend to an inn for food; as the friend leaves, he tells Eumenides his name: "I am Jack" (733). When they reach the inn, Eumenides is embarrassed to accept food he cannot pay for, but Jack urges him to look into his purse, which miraculously proves to be "full of money" (748). Eumenides joyfully sits down to feast and cheerfully agrees when Jack asks, "are you content I shall be halfes in all you get in your journey?" (759–60).

The scene shifts back to the magic well, and Huanebango's companion (Booby the Clown or "Corebus") and the ugly but kind daughter repeat the actions of Zantippa and Huanebango. This time, however, Celanta strokes and combs the magic head, which showers gold into her lap. Celanta then leads Booby-Corebus home, and he recites the lines of the old man's prophecy from the beginning of the play: "So Corebus things have well hit, / Thou hast gotten wealth to mend thy wit" (793–94).

The completion of this minor plot introduces the successive completions of all the others. Jack and Eumenides enter, now at Sacrapant's lair. Jack stuffs Eumenides' ears with wool "because you shall not be intised with his inchanting speeches" (800–801), and Sacrapant knows the end is near when he cannot cast his spell: "What, not a word but mum, / Then Sacrapant thou art betraide" (807–8). A now-invisible Jack removes Sacrapant's wreath and sword and declares "the Conjurer hee is dead, and vowes never to trouble us more" (818–19). Eumenides has to remove his earplugs before he can understand his friend, who instructs him to dig with Sacrapant's sword and reveal the magic light. As Jack explains: "so long as this light lasts, so long doth his arte indure, and this being out, then doth his arte decay" (828–29). Jack reminds us that only "she that is neither maide, wife, nor widowe" (836–37) can blow out the light, and he tell Eumenides to blow a horn (which has strangely appeared among the props on stage: the directions have not mentioned it before). The horn summons Venelia who breaks the glass and extinguishes the light. To help the audience recall the earliest events of the play, Jack explains to Eumenides: "this is she that ranne madding in the woods, his betrothed love that keepes the crosse, and nowe this light being out, all are restored to their former libertie" (839–42). Jack draws a curtain and reveals *"Delia . . . asleepe."* Eumenides exclaims, "Thou fairest flower of these westerne parts" (850) and awakens Delya. She immediately recognizes her proper husband: "My faith, my heart, my hand, I give to thee" (861). Meanwhile, Jack has apparently dragged Sacrapant's body offstage, for he returns with the conjurer's head and explains that it is an old man's head, "for maister, this Conjurer tooke the shape of the olde man that kept the crosse: and that olde man was in the likenesse of the Conjurer" (869–71). Eumenides blows the horn once more, and Delya's brothers appear, along with the reunited and rejuvenated Venelia and Erestus, the "old" man who was at the cross.

This joyous conclusion is momentarily interrupted when Jack reminds Eumenides of his promise to share everything equally. Of course, this oath means that Jack gets precisely "half" of Delya, and Eumenides honorably and sorrowfully prepares to kill her: "Content your selves," he tells her brothers, "my word is past to him, therefore prepare thy selfe Delya for thou must die" (901–2). Having tried his friend's constancy, Jack relents and asks, "Do you now remember since you paid for the burying of a poore fellow?" (905–6). This "Jack" is, of course, the "Jack" who was "a marvelous fellow," but too poor to be buried. As the stage direction says, *"Jacke leapes downe in the ground,"* returning to the grave his friend had purchased for him.

All the characters of Madge's tale leave the stage, and only the old wife herself and the two pages remain. She has fallen asleep, and Frolicke has to prompt her to explain that Eumenides' friend was "the ghost of the poore man, that they kept such a coyle to burie" (920–21). When Madge offers a "cup of ale and a tost," Fantasticke asks, "Then you have made an end of your tale Gammer?" (925). Her reply is slightly mysterious: "Yes faith: When this was done I tooke a peece of bread and cheese, and came my way, and so shall you have too before you goe, to your breakefast" (926–28). It has been suggested that this speech is partly directed toward the two pages and partly addressed to the audience, as an epilogue.[4] After answering Fantasticke's question ("Yes faith"), Madge turns to the audience and adopts the past tense, in fact a sequence of past tenses—"was done . . . tooke . . . came"—and then uses a future tense ("shall . . . have"). There is a hint here that she is turning away from the completed tale and from the time at which the tale took place (even further in the past than the stage-representation we have just seen) and is now predicting what the audience will do after they leave.

As this final little tantalizing puzzle suggests, the play has been rather carefully constructed to leave us quite convinced that "things that seeme are not the same" (160). Peele has even managed to finish the various plots in almost the reverse order of their introduction, since the opening sequence is pages and Madge/brothers/Erestus–old man–bear/Lampriscus's daughters/Huanebango and Booby/Eumenides/Jack and the closing sequence is Lampriscus's daughters, Huanebango, and Booby/Eumenides and Delya/Erestus and Venelia/brothers and Delya/Eumenides and Jack/pages and Madge. Although each strand has been introduced through the apparently fortuitous coincidence of the stolen princess and the old man being geographically near one another, the plots are eventually knit together quite satisfactorily: enchantments are lifted (Delya, brothers, Venelia, old man–bear–Erestus), lovers and family members united (brothers, Delya, Erestus, Venelia, the comic bridegrooms and their mates), and almost all the promises, prophecies, and "good" spells fulfilled. Usually, the audience has some verbal or visual reminder when a prediction is fulfilled (the old man's words repeated, or the little light blown out, for example) and Sacrapant's boasts and forbodings are also carefully interlocked with his final defeat.

Structural Flaws

While it is certainly true that no Elizabethan play of a comparable length has so complex a plot, it is even possible that no play of more generous dimensions comes close. The nearest approaches might be Greene's *James IV* and, less complex, Kyd's *Spanish Tragedy;* both plays have frame structures, and in *James IV* there is a crossover of characters from frame to "inner" play which reverses the way in which Madge's tale comes to life. Granted this complexity and the play's very short length, a literal reading of the plot, notebook in hand, will produce a few loose ends. Critics have settled on the following as their jointly favored list: the Delya and Venelia plots are too similar (both are what the folklorists call "abducted maiden" stories); Sacrapant seems to require a great deal of killing (wreath and sword removed; light blown out; head cut off); the two brothers do not blow out the light when they find it, despite the old man's advice; we do not know very precisely how Venelia fulfills the special conditions for the person who can extinguish the flame (neither maid, wife, nor widow); although Huanebango is condemned to be a "ravening pray to Crowes and Kites" (561), he ends up at the well and in Zantippa's care; the conclusions of the Zantippa-Huanebango and Celanta-Booby marriage plots are not exactly parallel; we never see the result of the disenchantment of Huanebango, Booby, Venelia (who never speaks), and the old man–Erestus (who says nothing at the end of the play).[5]

Several of these objections are merely personal preferences (the similar Delya and Venelia plots; the failure of Lampriscus's daughters to speak and act precisely the same); in one case Peele is criticized for being too schematic and in the other for not being schematic enough. Other objections again require Peele to write the critic's play and not his own. A scene in which Huanebango and Booby-

Corebus discover their new wives' true natures would be very funny, but it could hardly follow or interrupt the reunion of Delya and her brothers, her escape from death into Eumenides' affection, and Jack's departure for the underworld without seriously disturbing the lovely tonal and emotional balance of the play's present conclusion. Even Madge and the pages are chastened, albeit pleased, at the very end. A Huanebango who could hear Zantippa or a Booby-Corebus who could see Celanta do not fit the ending of *The Old Wives Tale.*

Among the other objections may be found some more interesting ones. The woman who is neither maid, wife, nor widow is a proverbial Elizabethan conundrum; perhaps we are meant to accept Venelia as a mute miracle, or to believe that her legal status is undefined because she has been betrothed to Erestus, slept with him, but has not yet married him in church.[6] Unless we become fascinated by the riddle and do not know some clever answer, this characterization only makes the play more mysterious and more magical. If a rational explanation has to be found for the brothers' failure to blow out the light when they discover it, then one could answer (a) they do not fit the riddle's conditions, and (b) they may themselves be magically prevented from harming the man who already has them under a spell,[7] and (c) if they did blow out the light and it does control Sacrapant's magic, the play would end too soon and with many more loose ends than it now has. When the furies place Huanebango next to the well of life, perhaps they do not know what they do: good prevails over evil in the play, and many good deeds in the play are done unthinkingly or without plan. Perhaps the furies expect crows and kites where only Zantippa and the well of life exist. Finally, it is true that several methods seem to be employed to kill Sacrapant, although any one would seem to be enough. When Jack removes the wreath and sword and later when he beheads Sacrapant, he fulfills the condition that the magician can die "but by a dead mans hand" (431); either act would seem to be sufficient, but Sacrapant is a mystifying, dangerous force, and one cannot be too careful.[8] Sacrapant's light must be extinguished not to kill him, but to end his enchantments; otherwise his "skill shall still endure" (427), apparently even after his death.

Dramatic Design

If we abstract ourselves from the plot's details, it is possible to detect a fair degree of shaping in the action. Although Madge and her two listeners remain on stage throughout the play, characters within her tale sometimes leave the stage, to be replaced by another group. These moments when the stage is cleared divide the play into quasi-scenes, and the pattern of this division illuminates Peele's design. The opening section introduces the frame-story, the lesser figures who search for Delya (her brothers, Huanebango, Booby), the important prophetic figure of the "old" man (Erestus), and the Zantippa-Celanta plot. The next section ends the suspense about Sacrapant by revealing him and showing the repulse of his first opponents, Delya's brothers (335–431). A short section at the play's very center (432–527) concerns the "hero," Eumenides, and his meeting with Erestus. The old man's prophecy for Eumenides, unlike his prophecies for other characters, immediately begins to be fulfilled when Eumenides pays for Jack's burial. The fourth section shows Sacrapant repelling another assault (Huanebango and Booby) and tormenting his earlier victims, Delya and her brothers. Now the play begins to resolve its multiple interests: the next section (611–86) shows Zantippa finding her mercifully deaf husband, Huanebango. At once, Jack and Eumenides form the team that will finally overthrow Sacrapant (687–768), and they share a ceremonial feast. Lampriscus's other daughter, Celanta, now finds her husband, who fulfills the prophecy he had heard from the old man (769–94), and the play's final section (795–914) resolves each of the remaining plots, returns us to the frame-story, and concludes the play.

This analysis shows how *The Old Wives Tale* concentrates on a perfectly appropriate folkloric conflict of good against evil, youth against age, generosity against mean-spiritedness. Peele withholds the principal challenger, Eumenides, for a long time and carefully frames his introduction with two spectacular demonstrations of Sacrapant's evil power (thunder, lightning, and two furies appear in each framing episode, while in the first Sacrapant also magically produces food, wine, and a Spanish friar). Since virtually all the play's characters visit the "white Beare of Englands wood" either in person or by proxy and since he regularly delivers a prediction to each visitor, we also sense the play's movement toward a conclusion as the predictions are gradually fulfilled. The fact that predictions *are* fulfilled also assures us—if the fairy-tale atmosphere did not—that Sacrapant's boastful confidence in his invincibility and immortality will somehow prove false, although we cannot anticipate (and presumably do not want to try to anticipate) precisely how the sorcerer will meet his match.

The rhythm which the prophecy-fulfillment pattern imposes on the play contributes to its sense of confidence and wonder. Although the audience cannot know precisely how everything will work out, we remain sure that it will. All our comic and sentimental anticipations are satisfied: brothers find sisters, men and women find their (carefully graduated) mates, and so on. This balance combined with suspense appears in the arrangement of characters as well as in the action. Erestus, the old-young man who is a bear by night, is clearly Sacrapant's mighty opposite. Although Erestus has suffered loss and labors under Sacrapant's enchantment, he has a prophetic power, a humility, and perhaps a Christian faith which makes him Sacrapant's near equal. The balance between the moral power of the "bear" and Sacrapant's evil is objectified when we learn (at the end of the play) that Erestus's aged appearance actually represents Sacrapant's true features and that Sacrapant's youthful features are truly Erestus's own face. A more limited version of the same transformation appears in Delya's forgetting of herself: she gets a new name and uses a goad to torture her brothers.

Peele balances the characters in another way: they often appear as interlocking opposites. The boastful, condescending Huanebango receives a shrewish, contemptuous wife, but then (presumably) regains his hearing to "enjoy" wedded bliss; kindly but stupid Corebus-Booby wins a sweet but ugly wife, but they share wealth (and perhaps magical protection from the friendly "head" in the well of life) to make their future secure. Talkative Erestus regains his silent Venelia. Even Eumenides' name (which means "the kindly ones" or "the gracious ones") has a part in the play's careful economy. Among the Greeks, "Eumenides" was a propitiary or euphemistic name for the furies, or Erinyes. Thus, Eumenides undoes the evil work of his namesake, Sacrapant's furies.

Beneath *The Old Wives Tale*'s flamboyant variety and often mesmerizing spectacle, we can detect the general pattern of classical and Elizabethan comedy. The action presses most of the characters toward the initial situation of the three pages' master, whom "Cupid hath led . . . to the faire Lady" (11–12), or as Frolicke earthily calls her, "his wench." Various obstacles are overcome so that in the end Jack and Jill finally get together. This comic model means, of course, that sex and sexual qualifications will be attached to most of the episodes in some way or another. Sacrapant has captured Delya, but she chastely resists capitulation. Her brothers cannot "rescue" her, because her rescue requires a sexual partner, the perfect mate, Eumenides. Almost casually, the play arranges that Huanebango and Zantippa and Booby-Corebus and Celanta should meet under conditions which allow them to ignore their respective disadvantages. The exotic qualification that permits Venelia to extinguish the magic light and free the cast of their enchantments is, of course, a sexual qualification. She participates and does not participate in all the sexual roles an Elizabethan woman ordinarily plays (maid, wife, widow). Even Jack enters this pattern because he represents a positive alternative, friendship and loyalty, to the married happiness Eumenides and Delya have almost achieved. The folklore motif from which his story comes—the so-called "grateful dead"—usually concludes with precisely the threat (dividing the lady equally and fatally) which concludes *The Old Wives Tale.* And the folklore story typically ends with the generous return of life to the living and the dead to the grave.[9]

These interpretations illustrate the play's extraordinarily capacious nature. For a very short play, it contains great variety. That variety includes many different social classes, many different literary models and folklore motifs, many different levels of language, many different theatrical effects—from song to apparitions and magic and feasting. Two other qualities help make *The Old Wives Tale* an extremely puzzling play. Along with variety, the audience must accept both frequent ellipsis and (the very opposite) frequent repetition. A clear example of the play's elusive nature is the casual, even reticent, handling of Venelia. While we may be able to accept her silence, for example, as part of the play's magical method, we may certainly feel that her qualifications as "neither wife, widow, nor maide" (429) have not been made clear. This puzzle is quite different from accepting that such a woman could (for an Elizabethan) exist; the point here is that the play does not tell us very directly how Venelia fits the description. At the same time, we may justly feel that the play hammers certain points excessively, as when one brother repeats the old man's prediction and the second brother echoes the repetition. Or again, the play emphasizes the little light's importance again and again, but not always in a way that makes the characters' attitudes toward it very lucid. Similarly, the old man's dual nature is twice discussed, and the two brothers are identified no fewer than three times.[10]

Dramatic Satire or Dramatic Folk Tale?

These three features—variety, elision, and redundancy—have helped to produce widely conflicting interpretations of what the play means and what it seeks to do in the theater. The two chief lines of modern criticism were established very early. In 1903, F. B. Gummere set the dominant critical response when he argued that Peele blended "romantic drama" (i.e., the folklore stories and the "wandering knight" tale) with "a realism which turns romance back upon itself."[11] A little later, Gwenan Jones rejected this view and held that *"The Old Wives' Tale . . .* is just what it purports to be, a straightforward representation of a folktale." Jones also offered a telling summary of Gummere's view when she wrote that his view treats the play as "a burlesque upon a certain type of drama, and that its faults are therefore not faults but his [Peele's] means of attaining his purpose."[12] That is, according to Gummere's argument, any flaws in *The Old Wives Tale*—omissions, logical gaps, the stuttering progress of the plot—in fact form part of Peele's deliberate crafting of the play. Other authors have developed Gummere's theory in a fascinating direction; they suggest that the qualities of the play which seem puzzling or aesthetically unappealing are in fact Madge's responsibility. Peele, they believe, conducts the play as Madge would have done had she continued to narrate the story, complete with repetitions, plot confusions, unexplained appearances and disappearances and so forth.[13] This argument does not necessarily make the play any better artistically (as Gummere generally tries to do), but it shifts the "blame" to Madge and asks us to admire Peele's cleverness in reproducing her muddled but engaging manner.

Whatever the value of these competing views, and they are very long-standing disagreements, the argument itself has two great merits: it turns us back to the play, asking how these contradictory interpretations could have arisen; and it implicitly asks us to consider the play's original audience. When we return to the play, one main drawback to Gummere's argument becomes clear: the play never invites us to judge its "realism." It alone establishes standards of logic, causality, behavior, and judgment. The theater audience does not become the ethical or social standard, as the court audience and especially Queen Elizabeth do in *The Araygnement of Paris* or in Lyly's court comedies, nor does *The Old Wives Tale* ostentatiously include various "levels" of reality.[14] Some episodes, like those involving Huanebango or Jack's tavern-mates, momentarily inject a version of life quite different from the pages, from Madge, or from Sacrapant, but these episodes quickly blend into the dominant romantic, magical, and folkloric patterns. To make the same point through analogy, we could say that *The Old Wives Tale* lacks the overarching Olympian level of Lyly's *Gallathea,* where the gods function as images of court power and court behavior. *The Old Wives Tale* comes to seem like a play restricted to the wood outside Athens in *A Midsummer Night's Dream* or the forest of Arden in *As You Like It,* without the contrasting (and hence measuring) Shakespearean elements such as Theseus and Hippolyta or Duke Frederick and his court.

The Old Wives Tale puzzles the critics because it constantly refers the audience back into the play and adduces its own private standards of what is real and unreal, likely and unlikely, true and false. To break into this "sealed" world, readers have suggested several external standards which may be used to explain the play. One interpretation holds that *The Old Wives Tale* satirizes earlier romantic plays about knights on quest, damsels in distress, and evil enchanters.[15] This view has not been very successful because few of these supposed plays have survived and because *The Old Wives Tale* has a very different effect from the few which do survive. A variant interpretation holds that the play was performed as an "afterpiece," but this argument is unprovable because no example of an afterpiece survives from the period.[16] The other main attempt to explain the play through some external set of facts regards it as a series of references to living Elizabethans.[17] This explanation cannot be dismissed *a priori,* but like the others it is a retreat from critical judgment, an attempt to find some factual scaffold which will define the play.

These interpretations are not in fact interpretations of the play, but of its relation to something else, and even if they are true, or partly true, they still offer little help with understanding *The Old Wives Tale* itself. If they send us back to the play with renewed interest, what do we find? As the description of the plot and the patterns of action suggested, it is possible to see *The Old Wives Tale* as a varied and exciting comedy. Its subjects are the simple and large subjects of many folk stories: love, risk, generosity, good and evil. It treats these subjects in a largely unpsychological manner and approaches issues of human emotion and values through many linked but separately superficial episodes and stories. As the critics have shown, asking logical questions about the plot will reveal some loopholes or inconsistencies. The same is true when we expect Eumenides or Sacrapant or Delya to display complex psychological attitudes or when we treat the play as if it were some dramatic Erestus, capable of answering our questions about life, love, knavery, and happiness. *The Old Wives Tale* cannot serve these functions. If we accept both its simplicity and its tightly controlled and inwardly directed standards, we may also accept John Crow's remark: "this play is utterly and completely unsophisticated."[18] This view echoes Gwenan Jones's judgment, although Crow seems to regard it as a criticism and Jones as praise.

Having identified *The Old Wives Tale* as a comedy using numerous folk motifs to describe human life and relations in the simplified terms folk stories employ, we can then reach our own verdicts on the value of such an enterprise. Two other features of the play deserve attention: the frame induction and the spectacular stage effects. Peele's frame is exceedingly "sophisticated" and virtually unparalleled in Elizabethan drama.[19] The "coming-to-life" of Madge's story is so surprising and so efficiently done that it reminds a modern audience of Luigi Pirandello's similar dramatic experiments. Perhaps the implicit contrast with Pirandello, who deliberately makes his plays highly intellectual, has led critics to expect that *The Old Wives Tale* will achieve intellectually the same extraordinary standard it sets technically. And yet, the contrast between the delightfully artificial construction of the play and its simple (but neither unintelligent nor unfeeling) vision of life provides great theatrical pleasure. This pleasure, along with the sheer fun and excitement of the stage effects, of the large cast, and of the complex plot, make *The Old Wives Tale* a compelling and very satisfying theater-piece. The noise and visual effects, like the folk tales themselves, may seem incongruous in the highly wrought frame structure, but they too provide great pleasure in the theater. Calling *The Old Wives Tale* a "show" may be meant to diminish its claim on our interest, but it is a description Peele would probably not have minded at all.[20] Moreover, the combination of high art and simplicity is one of the most cherished of all Elizabethan courtly values, as the period's salt cellars or miniatures or textile samplers amply demonstrate.

The Audience

This description of the play leads us to one final question: what was the nature of its Elizabethan audience? At first glance, the title page seems to provide a conclusive answer: it was "played by the Queenes Majesties players." This phrase identifies the Queen's Men, a public theater company that had been assembled in 1583.[21] Throughout their existence, they often toured in the provinces (a less costly activity than playing in a London theater), and Philip Henslowe records on 8 May 1594 that the company "brocke & went into the contrey to playe."[22] They do not reappear in London after this date. While the title page statement would seem to place the play in a London public theater during the late 1580s or early 1590s,[23] then, it is possible that the text we have represents a touring version, but it seems more likely that the text is indeed a full or almost full version playable only by a well-equipped metropolitan company.[24]

Yet, *The Old Wives Tale* seems very unlike other plays performed on the London public stage in the late 1580s or early 1590s. Although the printed text may not represent the play as it was performed in a specific theater, it certainly seems to envisage what is known as "simultaneous staging," where several different locations (for example, Sacrapant's lair, the well, the cross where Erestus stands) appear on stage at once.[25] This form of staging was much more common at court than on the public stage. Furthermore, the play has a large cast and seems to require a number of boy actors. Even assuming that a single actor might play more than one role, the play seems prodigal of its actors.[26] The spectacular dramaturgy would have been at home on either the public or the private/court stage. The large number of props again suggests a well-equipped troupe, or perhaps one which could call on the resources of the Queen's Office of the Revels.

Since we have no factual evidence of the play's original auspices, no certain conclusion is possible.[27] In addition to the points already reviewed, however, there are some others which are much less clear. For example, the play actually includes an "audience" (Madge and the pages); their attitudes might give us a glimpse of what the "real" audience was like. The pages certainly seem to come from a more sophisticated and urban social class than Madge and Clunch: they are trained singers, they can allude to classical gods and misquote Terence (line 10), and they are unaccustomed to night in the woods. Their attitude toward what they see can be debated: one critic finds it "uncomplicated and sympathetic acceptance," and another claims they "are wittily and ironically aware of the foolishness of the story."[28] The first estimate is probably more apt. The tone of the pages' very few speeches during the performance is hard to judge precisely, but their remarks sound like the comments of interested and pleased spectators, amused at the complexity and spectacle of the tale (e.g., lines 243–45, 254, 528–29). Like the contrast between the play's ingenious structure and its simple folkloric contents, the pages' attitude appears to be a truly Elizabethan combination of sophistication and simplicity. Peele has made their relation with Madge and Clunch a further example of the art which appears artless and thereby pleases the more.

If we consider the dramatic context of *The Old Wives Tale* more generally, the pages point toward a fairly sophisticated audience, for they recall the characters—like Rafe, Robin, and Dick in *Gallathea* (ca. 1585), or Dromio, Riscio, Halfpenny, and Lucio in *Mother Bombie* (ca. 1590)—who throng John Lyly's plays written for child performers at court or in private theaters. *The Old Wives Tale* may have other connections with Lyly's plays. Only two characters in the period's printed drama have the name "Eumenides": the hero of this play and the friend of the hero in Lyly's *Endymion or The Man in the Moon.*[29] Just when *Endymion* was first performed is unclear, but it was printed in 1591, and the identical names and chronological proximity, as well as the probability that Lyly and Peele were acquainted at Oxford and the fact that both were trying to find an audience in London in the 1580s and 1590s, suggest that there is some connection between the plays.[30] Whatever that connection may be, Lyly's court prologue (*Endymion* was presented before the queen) gives a valuable hint on the way we might approach *The Old Wives Tale:* "Most high and happy Princesse, we must tell you a tale of the Man in the Moone, which if it seeme ridiculous for the method, or superfluous for the matter, or for the meanes incredible, for three faultes wee can make but one excuse. It is a tale of the Man in the Moone."[31] This elegant excuse, which is no explanation at all, succinctly invites the sophisticated courtiers to enjoy the play both for its ridiculous and incredible nature and for the high artistry promised by the prologue itself.

When all this information and speculation is sifted, the evidence for the original audience and auspices of *The Old Wives Tale* proves just as confusing and contradictory as much else in the play. On balance, the play has many features we associate with court drama. At the same time, it covers a wider range of tastes, uses a wider range of dramatic and theatrical techniques, and offers a greater variety of subject matter and stances toward that subject matter than any other play of its period. Peele blended attitudes and values skillfully and made a play adaptable to both public and private or courtly performance. While this unusual mixture may produce a gallimaufry, as some critics charge, a sympathetic view will regard it as a unique fusion. It is Peele's only play to range through so many possible appeals to such diverse audiences. For once, an occasion or a commercial requirement or both led him to write a play which escapes the limit of any single audience or moment. The result is as mysteriously attractive as its own magical contents.

Chapter Five
The Battle of Alcazar and Elizabethan Politics

Some attractions of *The Battle of Alcazar* can be gleaned from the title page of the play's principal source. It begins simply enough: *The Second part of the booke of Battailes, fought in our age* (1587). The author, John Polemon, then offers his sources: "taken out of the best authors and writers in sundrie languages." Puffery finally takes over: "Published for the profit of those that practise armes, and for the pleasure of such as love to be harmlesse hearers of bloudie broiles."[1] The audience for the Admiral's Men certainly contained many lovers of "bloudie broiles," as the play's apparent survival for about a decade on the Elizabethan stage testifies.[2] Right from the start they could be assured of an exciting royal massacre:

> Sit you and see this true and tragicke warre,
> A modern [contemporary] matter full of bloud and ruth,
> Where three bolde kings confounded in their height,
> Fall to the earth contending for a crowne. . . . (49–52)

The three dead kings included two members of the Moroccan royal house, Abdelmelec and his usurping nephew Muly Mahamet ("the Moor"), and the king of Portugal, Sebastian.

Contemporary Importance of the Play

While politics and war in northern Africa might have only an exotic rather than a nationalistic interest for Elizabethans, Portuguese affairs were a very different matter. Sebastian himself descended from the English house of Lancaster, and with his death the direct succession to the Portuguese throne ended. His uncle, Don Henry, ruled briefly and ineffectually, but Philip II of Spain soon invaded the country. Elizabeth's policymakers and her subjects agreed in hating Spain; queen and people, therefore, happily backed a native Portuguese pretender, one Don Antonio. Antonio pressed his claims through an effective propaganda campaign which produced, among many other documents, another of the play's sources: *The Explanation. Of the True and Lawfull Right and Tytle, of the Moste Excellent Prince, Anthonie* . . . (1585). Published in English, French, and Latin, this short book circulated around Europe and shouted what every anti-Spanish government wanted to hear: Philip had betrayed Sebastian in order to gain Portugal for himself: "The King of *Castile* . . . not onelye denyed to performe his promise, but also (that is farre woorse) caused a proclamation to bee made . . . whereby all his subjectes were commaunded . . . that none . . . shoulde accompanye Kinge *Sebastian* in that Voyage" (sig. A2r). Although historically untrue, the conclusion seemed obvious: "no other conjecture [can] bee gathered [than] . . . that the King of *Castile* by his unmesurable ambition & insatiable desire to have dominion, neither coveted nor hoped for any other thing then [than] that king *Sebastian* . . . should be overthrown and come to destruction" (sig. A2r-v).[3] Thus, while Sebastian had died in 1578, Don Antonio kept the issue alive for another decade and more. Spanish imperial ambitions helped, of course; they produced both the nagging wars in the Low Countries and the Armada of 1588. Indeed, when England sought to revenge the Armada's attack, Don Antonio joined Drake and Norris in the ill-fated expedition of 1589, the same one Peele celebrated with his *Farewell*.[4] Political and romantic interest in the subject never flagged: in 1598, news reached England that a man claiming to be Sebastian himself had appeared with a marvelous (and utterly false) story of having survived the Battle of Alcazar. No fewer than four such claimants eventually appeared, and the legend retained enough power to inspire John Dryden's superb play *Don Sebastian* (1689).

Finally, history generously provided a further attraction: a native English legend died at Alcazar. Captain Thomas Stukeley (or "Stukley," as Peele usually names him) fits one modern stereotype of the adventurous Elizabethan freebooter.[5] Early in life he seems to have been on good terms with the government; later, however, Queen Elizabeth and Lord Burghley, her chief minister, turned against Stukeley, and he was ordered arrested. Stukeley managed to gain a temporary freedom and sailed to Spain. There he quickly became a dependent, perhaps even a favorite, of Philip II, who employed him as an emissary to the Pope. *The Battle of Alcazar* itself describes the end of Stukeley's career: his title, "marques . . . of Ireland" (462); his intended attack on Ireland; his eventual decision to join King Sebastian's madcap invasion of North Africa. Thus, the plains of Alcazar witnessed the deaths of "Three Kings that were, and One that would be fain."[6] Despite his Roman Catholicism and actions which might easily be called treasonous, Stukeley became a popular English hero. Numerous ballads about him appeared, the Admiral's Men performed a play called "stewtly" in late 1596 and early 1597, and references appear in other works.[7] He was even honored with a play, *The Famous History of the life and death of Captaine Thomas Stukeley,* which reached print in 1605.

The Battle of Alcazar's subject matter thus had many attractive features. The play could also count on two strong theatrical attractions: Edward Alleyn, the great tragic actor of the later 1580s and 1590s, took the role of the Moor, and the play exploits the recent success of Marlowe's *Tamburlaine the Great,* a two-part play in which Alleyn performed as Tamburlaine.[8] Just how Alleyn acted the part we cannot know, but he seems to have excelled at fustian roles like Tamburlaine and Orlando in Greene's *Orlando Furioso,* as well as potentially more subtle parts like Faustus in Marlowe's *Dr. Faustus.* Peele's play certainly gave Alleyn plenty of scope for furious and exciting (if rather monotonously violent and horrific) speeches. Watching the actor and the company that had produced *Tamburlaine,* Peele's audience would also have recognized his imitations of that spectacular success. High-flown speeches written in blank verse, an exotic locale, scenes of cruelty and violence—all these elements show Peele's attempt to overgo the earlier play, and one speech probably echoes Tamburlaine's last words:

> Convey Tamberlaine into our Affrike here,
> To chastice and to menace lawfull kings,
> Tamberlaine triumph not, for thou must die
> As Philip did, Caesar, and Caesars peeres. (222–25)[9]

The subject's and the play's attractions, then, were numerous: England's political interests, one of her gaudiest sons, a great actor, and the chance to imitate—perhaps to excel—Marlowe's immensely popular play. Precisely when *The Battle of Alcazar* was written, the theatrical source or auspices of the text we have, and indeed its author are all, however, questions open to dispute.[10] Peele's authorship rests on a few bits of inconclusive information: some lines from the play appear as his in an unreliable anthology, *Englands Parnassus* (1600), and most critics have assumed a connection in authorship and date between the play and Peele's *Farewell to . . . Norris and . . . Drake* (1589), which seems to contain an advertisement for *The Battle of Alcazar:*

> Bid Theaters and proude Tragaedians,
> Bid Mahomets Poo, and mightie Tamburlaine,
> King Charlemaine, Tom Stukeley and the rest
> Adiewe: to Armes, to Armes, to glorious Armes. . . . (20–23)

The very event this poem celebrates, a punitive expedition to Spain and Portugal that included Don Antonio the pretender, would have made the *The Battle of Alcazar* a good theatrical proposition, and the play generally contains the attitudes—by no means uniquely his—we expect of Peele: fervent nationalism, hatred of Spain, and so forth. The play's style, too, has Peelean qualities, especially if we allow for *Tamburlaine*'s influence. Thus, it has been generally agreed that Peele wrote the play (no other author has been suggested), and that it was composed after the publication of its main sources (1585 and 1587, respectively), after the Armada's defeat in August 1588, after the success of the two parts of *Tamburlaine,* and about the time (mid-1589) of the Norris–Drake–Don Antonio voyage to Spain and Portugal.

Although the title page claims "As it was sundrie times plaid by the Lord high Admirall his servants," the quarto printed in 1594 probably represents a cut text designed for a shorter than ordinary performance by a smaller than usual group of actors. Various features of the text suggest as much: it is quite brief (only about 1,452 text lines); it lists several characters in stage directions although they have no speaking parts (implying that their speeches have been cut); numerous speeches, especially long ones, break down grammatically and syntactically in ways that suggest they have been cut and patched or spliced together (see, e.g., lines 9–10, 688–91, 935–38, and the jumbled speeches and events in Act 5). Conclusive evidence that a fuller version once existed comes from the play's "plot." Very few "plots" survive from the Elizabethan period, but W. W. Greg has summarized their assumed nature and purpose: "theatrical 'plots' are . . . dramatic skeletons consisting primarily of the entrances and exits of the characters. . . . The object of the plots was evidently to remind actors and prompter of the sequence, dispositions, and requirements of the various scenes. . . ."[11] The "plot" of *The Battle of Alcazar* apparently comes from a revival in the period April 1598 to February 1599, or even later, and it demonstrates that a more complete *Battle of Alcazar* once existed.[12] Given its purpose, the plot offers most help with reconstructing stage action (especially the dumb shows), but no assistance in recovering the spoken lines cut from the play before it reached print. Compared with the plot, the 1594 text severely reduces the women's parts, probably because the acting company—perhaps dispersed outside London—lacked boys to speak the roles.[13] Other changes permit a performance using less scenic equipment, and Sebastian's role seems to have been shortened in several places. Once allowance has been made for the hypothetical origin and history of the 1594 version, we may agree with Greg that "the text preserved to us in the Quarto is in the main a sound one."[14] Despite certain evident cuts, then, it seems unlikely that the truncated *Battle of Alcazar* makes a very different impression from the longer version Peele originally wrote and the Admiral's Men performed "sundrie times."

As the plot testifies, the 1594 quarto retains the structure—the sequence of events, introduction of characters, distribution of staged and narrated action—of the hypothetical long version.[15] Historically and dramatically, these events are extremely confusing, in part because Peele and his sources treat Moroccan proper names inconsistently and in part because Peele sought to compress and rearrange the historical events and relationships. Peele realized his audience's likely confusion: the Presenter rehearses events leading up to the play and then almost immediately Abdelmelec repeats the information (lines 119ff.) when he justifies his war on Muly Mahamet, "the Moor." As an added difficulty, Peele—or the play's reviser—made a few errors of fact.

Dramatic Structure

The play's action originates in a struggle for succession. An earlier ruler named Muly Mahamet Xeque decreed that his four sons—Abdallas, Abdelmunen, Abdelmelec, and Muly Mahamet Seth—should succeed him and one another, the eldest son first. Abdallas succeeded his father, but sought to place his own son, Muly Mahamet (usually called "the Moor"), on the throne. Inaccurately but very dramatically, Peele makes the Moor responsible for murdering his own two (unnamed) brothers and his uncle, Abdelmunen. So much the play's opening speech and dumb shows convey. Since Abdallas and Abdelmunen are both dead and the Moor has seized the throne, the central action concerns Abdelmelec's and later Muly Mahamet Seth's successful attempts to remove and punish their usurping nephew, the Moor. Although Abdelmelec conducts most of the campaign and is presented throughout as a virtuous and admirable king, he dies midway through the play's final battle and is, properly, followed by Muly Mahamet Seth, the undisputed ruler at the play's end.[16]

Abdelmelec defeats the Moor almost at once (lines 252ff.), and the Moor's search for revenge draws King Sebastian and Thomas Stukeley into the play. Describing his aim as "holy christian warre(s)" (635, 704), Sebastian eagerly agrees to help the Moor. Stukeley, sailing "To Ireland by pope Gregories command" (395) to foment rebellion against Queen Elizabeth, takes temporary shelter in Lisbon harbor. Sebastian's grandiloquent praise of Elizabeth (lines 667ff.) and equally grand descriptions of his "holy christian warre" fire Stukeley's own ambition. He agrees "To die with honor for Sebastian" (712). However glorious Sebastian's and Stukeley's designs, neither of their supposed allies—the Moor and Philip II—means to keep his promises (see lines 524ff. and 806ff.). Working with three dramatic locales—Lisbon, the Moor's mountain retreat, and Abdelmelec's royal court—Peele then develops the Moor's emotional frenzies, Abdelmelec's staunch and noble attempts to avoid war with Portugal, and Sebastian's pell-mell refusal to be denied his military glory. After a fine midnight council of war (lines 1064ff.), the final battle takes place at Alcazar. Abdelmelec rather abruptly dies of a previously undisclosed illness, but his courtiers pretend he is still alive, and Muly Mahamet Seth takes command of the loyal Moroccan forces. Sebastian (we are told, but not shown) dies in the battle, and we see Stukeley's own Italian soldiers murder him when they realize that the Christian forces have been conclusively defeated. Attempting to flee, the Moor drowns in the river Larissa, which had formed one of the Christian army's strategic defenses. Muly Mahamet Seth succeeds his brother and arranges proper burial for

Sebastian and a grotesque, if condign, desecration of the Moor's corpse.

John Yoklavich is probably right to praise *Alcazar*'s structure. Certainly Peele has organized and condensed the dangerously rambling source materials in a way neither he (in *Edward I*) nor Marlowe (in *Tamburlaine*) did.[17] His principal problem was how to diversify and enliven the period between Abdelmelec's original defeat of the Moor and the concluding battle at Alcazar. Several scenes usefully develop Abdelmelec's goodness and the Moor's extravagant vainglory and villainy, but Sebastian and Stukeley, with a dash of anti-Hispanic propaganda, provide the best possible diversion. Nor are the Stukeley and Sebastian scenes mere filler. Peele justifies their scenes as representing the European involvement in the North African struggle for succession. To understand the play's organization, we need to remember its title: the action leads inevitably to a single event whose outcome the audience already knows.[18]

The play's act-division can help us determine Peele's plan.[19] The first act establishes the conflict for succession, and the Moor's defeat forces him into exile. The second act reveals the gathering of outside forces to help the two sides: the Turks will support Abdelmelec (2.1); Stukeley arrives in Lisbon and declares he has "No thought . . . That workes not everie waie to win a crowne" (2.2); the Moor decides to seek King Sebastian's aid, although he plans to break the alliance as soon as possible (2.3); the triple alliance of Sebastian-Stukeley-Moor is agreed in Lisbon (2.4). Now the external forces gather their strength. Sebastian seeks help from Philip II, but we learn—through Stukeley's typically English but unhistorical suspicions—that this help may be false, just as Muly Mahamet intends his to be (3.1). Abdelmelec's noble compassion for his Portuguese enemy confirms our dismay at Spanish perfidy (3.2). In the act's last two scenes, we move to Tangier, where the Portuguese governor awaits his master, although Spanish help has now been recognized as false (3.3), and the two allies—one trusting and duped, the other sly and insincere—meet for the first time (3.4).[20] In the last scene of Act 3, the Moor pledges his son to Sebastian as a guarantee of the alliance, just as Ruben Archis had pledged her son to the Turkish Sultan to seal that alliance among the Moor's enemies (2.1). Act 4 has two brief scenes of military preparation. Abdelmelec easily commands his forces and pities Sebastian (4.1). Meanwhile, the Portuguese army leaders worry about their troops' loyalty and the wisdom of doing battle; the Moor's obsession with revenge leads him to deceive his allies once again (4.2). Finally, in one rather choppy and unsatisfying scene, we watch the battle and its aftermath (5.1).[21]

The play's shape seems reasonably clear: as Werner Senn claims, "The impulse in both camps . . . is an undisguised quest for sovereignty."[22] Indeed, this "quest" includes Philip II (in Peele's anti-Spanish treatment) and Stukeley, who would rather be "King of a mole-hill . . . Than the richest subject of a monarchie" (465–66). For Stukeley, Morocco replaces Ireland as a suitable arena for glory: "Saint George for England, and Irelande nowe adue, / For here Tom Stukley shapes his course anue" (735–36). Ambition and its associated deceit (in the Moor and Philip and even in Sebastian, who plans some form of religious crusade) motivate the major characters' actions and fill their speeches. It seems an excessive nicety to think that "revenge"—the word and idea that fill Abdelmelec's and the Moor's speeches—can be divided from ambition. Muly Mahamet's revenge is soured ambition: one motive decays into the other. Moreover, had Peele not chosen to make Abdelmelec the pious executor of Moroccan law, even his unwearying pursuit of the Moor could have been described as vengeful.

The Presenter, Dumb Shows, and Seneca

One of Peele's structural devices, the Presenter, deserves closer attention. This character links *The Battle of Alcazar* with Peele's dramaturgy elsewhere, and he also suggests that this play, like many others, may owe a debt to Seneca. The Presenter, familiar from civic shows like Peele's *Descensus Astraeae,* combines the function of an interpreter of spectacles (the presenter's role in pageants) with the function of a chorus in a classical play or in the various English plays modeled on Seneca. Not only does Peele use a presenter for the first time in English drama, he also makes an innovative use of the dumb show or pantomime.[23] Before and after *The Battle of Alcazar,* many plays employ allegorical dumb shows like those preceding Acts 2 and 5, but using characters from the main play in the initial dumb show appears to be Peele's invention. Later, introducing Acts 3 and 4, he mixes human characters with symbolic beings (Nemesis, Death, Furies) and symbolic props such as *"Dead mens heads in dishes."*

Peele exploits the Presenter and his dumb shows to great advantage. By regularly bringing the Presenter before the audience, Peele shapes a drama from his historical source. He compresses complex and potentially distracting events into narrative: the preliminary murders and some subsequent skirmishes, for example, or Sebastian's negotiations with Philip II and the voyage from Portugal to Africa. Through the Presenter's speeches, Peele also alerts the audience about important scenes to come—"imagine . . . this barbarous Moore . . . lives forlorne among the mountaine shrubs, / And makes his food the flesh of savage beasts" (307, 309–10, anticipating lines 537–61)—and tries to shape our attitudes toward the play's characters and actions—

> But ware ambitious wiles and poisned eies,
> There was nor aide of armes nor marriage,
> For on his waie without those Spaniardes king Sebastian went. (756–58)

Should any member of the audience miss the point, the Presenter will intervene to make sure we admire Sebastian: "Let fame of him no wrongfull censure sound, / Honour was object of his thoughtes, ambition was his ground" (989–90). The Presenter can also serve as a blunt guide to the play's structure; before Sebastian appears, the Presenter prepares the way: "Now listen lordings now begins the game, / Sebastians tragedie in this tragicke warre" (327–28).

Kyd's *Spanish Tragedy* and earlier Senecan and classically influenced plays would have prepared Peele's audience for the Grand Guignol of Nemesis, Furies, ghosts, and bleeding bones in *Alcazar*'s symbolic dumb shows. Here again Peele shows superior technique: the gruesome machinery does more than thrill the audience. Given the hyperbolic frenzy in the Moor's speeches, the dumb shows actually objectify his violent imagery and fevered imagination.[24] After the Moor has demanded that

> Some foule contagion of the infected heaven,
> Blast all the trees, and in their cursed tops,
> The dismall night raven and tragike owle
> Breed . . . (474–77)

or prayed,

> You bastards of the night and Erybus,
> Fiends, Fairies, hags that fight in beds of steele,
> Range through this armie with your yron whips,

> Drive forward to this deed this christian crew,
> And let me triumph in the tragedie,
> Though it be seald and honourd with my bloud,
> Both of the Portugall and barbarous Moore,
> Ride Nemisis, ride in thy firie cart,
> And sprinkle gore amongst these men of warre,
> That either partie eager of revenge,
> May honor thee with sacrifice of death . . . (1136–46),

the appearance of Nemesis, the Furies, Death, or *"Three ghosts crying* Vindicta" confirms this world's particular moral and psychological architecture. Nor do the Presenter's speeches and dumb shows manifest the Moor's imagery alone. When the Presenter describes how "Nemisis upon her doubling drum . . . Larumes aloud into Alectos eares" (288, 290), we hear echoes of Rubin Archis's promise:

> Of death, of bloud, of wreake, and deepe revenge,
> Shall Rubin Archis frame her tragicke songs,
> In bloud, in death, in murther and misdeede,
> This heavens mallice did begin and end. (162–65)

Her brother-in-law Abdelmelec continues the vengeful metaphor: "these rights {rites} . . . Have pearst by this to Plutos grave below, / The bels of Pluto ring revenge amaine" (166–68). Since Sebastian and Stukeley often give honor or fame as a motive, it is only fitting that the last dumb show should respond with *"Enter Fame like an Angell."* Thus, the dumb shows cease to be allegorical commentaries on dramatic events and move toward being ominous realizations of the hopes, fears, ambitions, and metaphors of the characters themselves. This quality makes the mingling of human and symbolic figures in some of the shows more plausible and powerful: metaphysical abstractions grow toward a terrible and destructive physical reality.

Although the Presenter seems in charge of the dumb shows, it strains credulity (and the text) to try too hard to "identify" the figure himself.[25] Like the dumb shows, he stands outside the play proper. The dumb shows elaborate distant and divine and infernal forces operating in the play's metaphysical realm; the Presenter stands "between" the audience and the play. While his words usually seem to be commentary, his speeches occasionally imply his personal, quasi-creative responsibility—"this tyrant king, / Of whome we treate" (14–15), for example. He certainly addresses the play's characters—"Thus Muly Mahamet is a counsell held, / To wreake the wrongs and murthers thou hast done" (305–6)—and he often speaks to the audience (e.g., lines 22, 30, 284, 327–28, 756–58, 989–90). The Presenter serves in a traditional commentator's role, and some speeches are the chorus's typical scene-setting lines (e.g., 1185ff.: "Mondaie the fourth of August seventie eight . . .") which appear in many later plays. When all allowances have been made, however, this Presenter remains an unusual figure, very characteristic of Peele's dramaturgy. He has analogies, for instance, with the speaker who opens *David and Bethsabe* and with Madge in *The Old Wives Tale.*

Using the Presenter, Peele manages some very striking effects. He apparently compares his audience to the Moor's original, mute victims: "Like those that were by kind of murther mumd, / Sit downe and see what hainous stratagems / These damned wits contrive" (21–23). Silencing the audience, the Presenter compares them to the Moor's victims who are "mummed," silenced, by their relative.[26] Thus we understand that the play means to touch our emotions as well as our intellect. Watching the play, we experience, imaginatively, its events. A few lines later, the Presenter warns, "Saie not these things are faind [feigned], for true they are" (30); Peele conventionally declares that the feigned representation—the performance just begun—is also "true." Finally, the Presenter offers some proverbial summing up as the final battle begins: "Bloud will have bloud, foul murther scape no scourge" (1168).[27] He moralizes on human mutability: "Ay me, that kingdomes may not stable stand" (1182), but concludes with appropriate, bloodthirsty exhortation: "Geve eare and heare how warre begins his song, / With dreadfull clamors, noise, and trumpets sound" (1192–93).

The Presenter's dumb shows and the language of the Moor's speeches they so often reflect, along with some other qualities such as a "deterministic tone," led P. H. Cheffaud to argue that *The Battle of Alcazar* manifests a *"double dépendance"* on Marlowe and on Seneca.[28] In his search for a theatrically salable product, Cheffaud finds, Peele combined two popular styles and methods: the chronicle history play and the Senecan "revenge" play. How we label the play and discriminate among its antecedents depends, of course, on relative criteria for "influence." No doubt the play has some Senecan elements, but if we appeal to a contemporary Elizabethan view, those elements do not seem very prominent. The Induction to *A*

Warning for Fair Women (printed in 1599) contains a reasonably just recipe for an English Senecan tragedy in the 1590s:

> How some damn'd tyrant to obtain a crown
> Stabs, hangs, impoisons, smothers, cutteth throats:
> And then a Chorus, too, comes howling in
> And tells us of the worrying of a cat:
> Then, too, a filthy whining ghost,
> Lapt in some foul sheet, or a leather pilch,
> Comes screaming like a pig half stick'd,
> And cries, *Vindicta!*—Revenge, Revenge![29]

Division into five acts, a supposedly classical device, and ghosts crying *Vindicta,* as three of Peele's do at the opening of Act 2, hardly constitute strong evidence for the play's Senecanism. Dumb shows precede each act of *Gorboduc* (1565) and the Senecan *Misfortunes of Arthur* (1587), for example, but the former play emphasizes a national and familial curse (almost a Senecan signature) and the latter uses a ghost to incite action and requires a very Senecan messenger. Both plays employ a figure named "Chorus" to mark the ends of each act and to moralize on the plays' subjects. By the criteria these plays establish or by those mentioned in the admittedly hostile lines from *A Warning for Fair Women, The Battle of Alcazar* has few Senecan qualities and even fewer which contribute significantly to its interest.

Still, Peele knew Terence and certainly Seneca in Latin as well as through contemporary English imitations and plagiarisms; Gager, moreover, tells us Peele had translated at least one Greek play. Thus, *The Battle of Alcazar*'s superior control over its fractious historical subject might derive indirectly from classical drama. Peele largely avoids having to use messengers to relate offstage and capacious actions. It is also possible that the Moor derives to some extent from the Senecan tyrant-villain, whose speeches often rant and bellow in Peele's manner. Yet, Marlowe's *Tamburlaine* could have taught his emulators that much about popular taste, and the infernal world which the play conceives very classically could derive from Vergil (lines 1169–71 allude to *Aeneid* IV, 696–700) or Ovid (apparently alluded to in line 273) as much as from Seneca or from the Senecan material in a play like Kyd's *Spanish Tragedy.* Aaron the Moor, in *Titus Andronicus,* is often cited as a "Senecan" character who resembles the Moor in *The Battle of Alcazar,* but Aaron, like Muly Mahamet, owes much to Marlowe and much to native English dramatic practice.[30] On balance, Peele's commercial acumen may have given his play a veneer of crowd-pleasing effects which ultimately derive from Seneca's plays, but *Tamburlaine* is a much larger creditor. The rest of *The Battle of Alcazar* can reasonably be given to Peele's native talent.

Polemon's *Second booke of Battailes* provided Peele his African and Portuguese material arranged in approximately chronological order, and Seneca (or his English imitators) may have contributed some rhetorical purple and some structural help. When critics have looked at the result, hoping to find logical causation or thematic unity, they have settled on the Moor's "crime" for the first and "revenge"—usually attributed to Seneca—for the second.[31] In a sense, the two must be combined to serve as the action's source, since the crime remains a single act without consequences until Abdelmelec responds with actions he calls "revenge." Even so, these opposed terms (crime, revenge) do not explain why the play continues beyond the Moor's initial defeat. To put the problem another way, the action's logical cause seems to shift from crime/revenge to revenge/revenge. Relentless talk of revenge and of Nemesis, "goddesse and deviser" (1158) of revenge, make that topic an attractive focus for the action, either as cause or thematic center. Peele often does organize his plays and pageants as a series of vignettes or scenes illustrating a single and perhaps "unifying" topic, such as revenge, loyalty, political sin, and so forth. Revenge appears as a motive, endlessly repeated and elaborated, for both the Moor and his uncle, Abdelmelec. Sebastian and Stukeley, however, serve only as accessories to revenge and never admit it as a motive. Nor, in fact, do they regard Nemesis as an all-powerful influence. They attribute their fates to fortune, the stars (lines 1363–64, 1370), God's displeasure (lines 916–19), and treachery (lines 1261–63). A motive, especially one shared or acknowledged by only two of the four principal characters, does not make a very satisfactory center around which to organize the play. Nor, of course, does revenge correctly describe the action's origin, although it fuels the Moor's and Abdelmelec's subsequent conflict.

Royal Succession and Elizabethan Politics

Despite the many vivid, melodramatic invocations of revenge, one subject receives even more comment: succession. The play's opening lines hammer again and again at the issue of Muly Mahamet Xeque's strange (to English eyes) command that his four sons should succeed one another in descending order of their ages. Primogeniture—inheritance by the eldest son to the exclusion of any brothers—determined many Elizabethan Englishmen's lives. Royal succession through the eldest son, his son, and so on, was utterly ingrained. In English public life, failure of the male line could produce such worrying claimants as Mary, Queen of Scots (executed in 1587), and a plethora of strong sons (the problem Muly Mahamet Xeque faced) had initiated the Wars of the Roses.[32] Thus, Peele had to present numerous confusingly named foreign monarchs and princes, and he also had to establish an exceedingly novel pattern of inheritance. Once the audience understands that the Moor claimed the throne as his father's son and that, moreover, his father had passed the throne to him rather than to his uncle, the Moor's title and anger might well have seemed justified. The words "rightfull" and "lawfull" appear over and over again, applied to both Abdelmelec and the Moor. Abdelmelec is called "lawfull true succeeding seed" (98) and claims that he is the "lawfull true succeeding prince" (147). Yet the Moor is "Abdallas lawfull seed" (250), "the true succeeding prince" (970, 1402) who makes "rightfull warre" (977). The opening 200 lines or so repeatedly call Muly Mahamet "traitor king" (25, 42, 108, 140) or "usurper" (283) or "Traitor and bloudie tyrant both at once" (138), but Abdelmelec, too, is a "traitor" (1113), a "traitor king" (1149), one of "those / That climbe aloft by force, and not by right" (939–40). To validate Muly Mahamet's position even further, King Sebastian accepts the Moor's legal title and vows "Sebastian lives to right his wrong" (622). The vocabulary and the issue were familiar to English audiences and would become even more familiar as the queen aged and adamantly refused to name her successor. Peele himself took up the legitimacy of Elizabeth's succession in *Anglorum Feriae* and, allusively, in *Edward I.*

Unfamiliar Moroccan political customs and public anxiety over Elizabeth's successor cannot, of course, make the Moor an admirable figure. Indeed, Peele virtually invented a stock character of the later drama, the "Moor-villain" who combines, as Eldred Jones says, "the grandiloquent extrovert and the subtle plotter."[33] Despite his sometimes monotonous rant, the Moor's character has dramatic nuance, and Peele uses the Moor-Abdelmelec struggle to reinforce a contrast in their natures. This contrast and the need to remind the audience of the political and military conflict led Peele to introduce a short Abdelmelec scene into each act, usually as the opening scene (Acts 1, 2, 4, and 5). These ceremonial glimpses present Abdelmelec as an utter contrast to his nephew: calm, deliberative, frank, gracious, compassionate, and loyal to his large family. While Abdelmelec always appears in formal scenes of victory, greeting, and courtly deliberation, Peele shows Muly Mahamet in both private, family scenes and more public, political moments. Consequently, the audience may formulate a sense of the Moor's character—his "habit of dodging reality,"[34] for example—while Abdelmelec remains more generalized if more "admirable."

Drama and Pageantry

An extraordinary scene shows the Moor's grandiose attempt to comfort his wife, Calypolis. Abdelmelec has redeposed the usurper and driven him to "some unhanted [isolated, unpeopled] place" (269) where he "lives forlorne among the mountaine shrubs, / And makes his food the flesh of savage beasts" (309–10). Hunted and dying of hunger, Calypolis begs that her husband "turne all curses"—his typical response—"to submisse complaints, / And those complaints to actions of reliefe" (486–87). Calypolis will not accept, as her son does, the reassurance that the Moor has deceitfully inveigled King Sebastian's aid: "more dishonor hangs on such misdeeds, / Than all the profit their returne can beare" (531–32). Muly Mahamet grandiosely promises, "be content, thy hunger shall have end, / Famine shall pine to death and thou shalt live" (503–4: the metaphor is striking). He shortly returns *"with flesh upon his sworde:"*

> Hold thee Calypolis feed and faint no more,
> This flesh I forced from a lyonesse,
> Meate of a princesse, for a princesse meate,
> . . . .
> Feede then and faint not faire Calypolis. . . . (537–39, 548)

Shakespeare, Jonson, and other dramatists thought this last line (later repeated twice in a speech of only twenty-five lines) hilarious, and they mocked it mercilessly. To be worth mocking, the speech—like the famous and mocked passages from *Tamburlaine* or *The Spanish*

Tragedy—had first to be memorable, even impressive. Edward Alleyn probably made it both.

Modern readers may discover too much sophistication in the Calypolis–Muly Mahamet contrast,[35] and in any case Calypolis disappears from the 1594 quarto after this scene. Nonetheless, Peele uses her patient, honorable suffering as a measure of both the Moor's character and his language. Her practicality does not necessarily undermine that bombastic speech; the Moor's son, for example, remains thoroughly enthusiastic. Rather, we see the Moor's attitude as one response, perhaps even an "heroic" one, among several possible reactions.

Like Calypolis, Abdelmelec provides a contrast with the Moor's cowardly craft. Abdelmelec pities his nephew's dupe, Sebastian, and tries to save the headstrong king:

> But for I have my selfe a souldier bin,
> I have in pittie to the Portugall
> Sent secret messengers to counsell him. (835–37)

Even on the threshold of battle, Abdelmelec can sigh, "Alas good king, thy fore-sight hath bin small" (1004). Noble, generous, defending his "right," Abdelmelec thus becomes a contrasting figure not only for the Moor, but for Sebastian and, indeed, for Sebastian's other deceitful ally, Philip of Spain. Peele draws Stukeley into the play through Sebastian, and through Sebastian Stukeley becomes part of the intricate network of contrasts and parallels. The Englishman senses, sooner than any other Christian, Philip's deception, but he never penetrates the Moor's insincerity. Sebastian and Stukeley, of course, also have very different motives from the Moroccan characters. Sebastian's hot-headed crusading and Stukeley's ambitious belief that his "deserts shall counterpoise a kings" (460) threaten to dissolve the central acts into incoherence. Here again the implicit contrasts with Abdelmelec (whom no European character ever confronts) and the explicit contrasts with Muly Mahamet (in the ceremonial meeting of 3.4 or the war-council of 4.2) hold the divergent interests together.

Despite, perhaps because of, this pattern of contrasts, Abdelmelec remains a wooden figure, more interesting as a corpse than as a living king, less glamorous than Stukeley or Sebastian, less vivid than the Moor.[36] Yet Abdelmelec fits very well into the play's design. If we look to revenge as a unifying theme, Abdelmelec may become "the instrument of Nemesis,"[37] while the Moor struggles to dominate the dangerous goddess, but both characters are more interesting when we consider them as political and dramatic contrasts. A political pattern, the succession crisis, works its way into the many character contrasts. This design allows Peele to meld some superficially digressive motivations and irrevelant incidents into a fair harmony.

Even setting aside the issue of the play's shape, many critics have found it undramatic. Seeking dramatized conflict, they find only static pageantry.[38] To some extent, *The Battle of Alcazar* recalls *The Araygnement of Paris:* there, too, a series of parallels and contrasts seldom produces confrontation. Indeed, the audience must first recognize the logical, emotional, political, or other relationships and then uncover their implied focus. When Abdelmelec dies during the battle of Alcazar, his brother decides to deceive the army:

> in this apparell as he dyed
> My noble brother will we heere advance
> And set him in his chayre with cunning props,
> That our Barbarians may beholde their King
> And thinke he doth repose him in his Tent. (1242–46)

A spectacular moment on stage, no doubt, and it serves as an image for Peele's dramaturgy elsewhere. Stiff formality and heavily ritualized scenes substitute for conflict among the characters or for a single character's introspection. Most debates or hints of debate quickly become occasions for exhortation. Thus, King Sebastian does not really argue Stukeley into joining his crusade; instead, the King "persuades" Stukeley against going to England when he delivers a long and loving paean to Queen Elizabeth (lines 667ff.). For Stukeley, apparently, as for Peele's audience, Elizabeth's dignity, grandeur, and power were all "reasons"—but not logical ones and not logically presented or debated—to give up the attack on Ireland.

Whatever the Admiral's Men might muster for gorgeous and exotic "oriental" splendor in costumes, props, and stage devices could also contribute to the ceremonial and formalized effects. The opening stage direction of Act 1, scene 2—"*Enter the Moore in his Chariot, attended* . . ."—probably conceals a very striking stage picture. In the final dumb show, a star blazes ominously and royal crowns drop mechanically from Fame's tree. This latter episode aims to show that the play's events have been foredoomed; a patterned, ritualized stage action imitates the shaping of human destinies by Fortune, or Nemesis, or other suprahuman forces.

As the Calypolis-Moor scene demonstrates, there are exceptions to the pageantlike presentation. Elsewhere, too, the play quickens into activity. When Stukeley argues with the Bishop (who wants to pursue the Irish expedition) and then twits him as the "reverent lordly bishop of saint Asses" (432), he momentarily sounds like the ribald and vivacious character of legend, and we have one of the few hints that his decision to go to Africa is opposed and that it requires any self-questioning. A more extended example occurs just before the final battle, when the Christian leaders gather in a powerful night-time council of war. Sebastian's opening speech avoids his usual and simplistic patriotic fervor and begins with sarcasm:

> Why tell me Lords, why left ye Portugall,
> And crost the seas with us to Barbarie,
> Was it to see the countrie and no more,
> Or else to fly before ye were assaild? (1064–67)

Abdelmelec's "messages to counsell quietnes" (1074; see lines 835–37) have clearly had an effect, and Sebastian's subordinates want to withdraw. The King then develops his usual line of glory-seeking exhortation:

> Cast feare aside, my selfe will leade the way,
> And make a passage with my conquering sword
> Knee deepe in bloud of these accursed Moores. . . . (1079–81)

The last line recalls the Moor's early promise:

> Such slaughter with my weapon shall I make,
> As through the streame and bloudie chanels deepe,
> Our Moores shall saile in ships and pinnaces,
> From Tanger shore unto the Gates of Fesse. (243–46)

Of course, Sebastian and the Moor have some similarities, and the Duke of Avero responds to his king in much the way Calypolis responded to her husband:

So well become these words a kingly mouth
That are of force to make a coward fight,
But when advice and prudent fore-sight
Is joyned with such magnanimitie,
Trophes of victorie and kingly spoiles
Adorne his crowne, his kingdome, and his fame. (1087–92)

Although couched in a courtier's smooth rhetoric, this speech clearly means that Avero, like Abdelmelec (see line 1004), does not believe that Sebastian has joined "prudent fore-sight" with his admirable royal courage. Before Sebastian can reply, Hercules—one of Stukeley's captains—enters to report "A hugie companie of invading Moores" (1094); he advises "Best then betimes t'avoide this gloomie storme, / It is in vaine to strive with such a streame" (1097–98).

Fearing that these doubts will sway Sebastian, the Moor now comes "uncalde" (1099) to stiffen his wavering ally. He succeeds in shaming Sebastian and the others, although he has to lie about the disloyalty of Abdelmelec's troops. Avero's and Stukeley's final speeches acknowledge that they still have many doubts about the battle, but pride and fame demand they fulfill their pledges. After the Christians leave, the Moor delivers a powerful soliloquy. He acknowledges his deceit—"Now have I set these Portugals aworke, / To hew a waie for me unto the crowne" (1133–34)—and admits that winning or losing the battle means less than destruction itself:

let me triumph in the tragedie,
Though it be seald and honourd with my bloud,
Both of the Portugall and barbarous Moore,
Ride Nemisis, ride in thy firie cart,
And sprinkle gore amongst these men of warre,
That either partie eager of revenge,
May honor thee with sacrifice of death. . . . (1140–46)

He ends by cursing Abdelmelec: "Damnd let him be, damnd and condemnd to beare / All torments, tortures, plagues and paines of hell" (1159–60).

Here, for once, the underlying conflicts among the characters and even within one camp rise into the dialogue. If we think of drama as conflict—the clash of ideas, values, and motives—then this scene is one of the play's dramatic moments. The Moor's concluding speech also gives us a rare opportunity to understand his nihilism, his drive for gory destruction no matter the cost or the victor. Conflict and introspection occur so infrequently, however, that they cannot be considered Peele's principal dramatic method. He could write scenes like this one, or the Calypolis-Moor argument, but he seems to have preferred pageantry and implicit contrast. Still, the night-council scene is good enough to make us wish to have a more complete text than the 1594 quarto provides.

Conclusion

A summary evaluation of *The Battle of Alcazar* must first acknowledge its place in contemporary Elizabethan political and theatrical history. It responds very directly to recent international events (the Armada, Portuguese affairs, English support for Don Antonio), but its structural focus on the royal succession also echoes an English audience's anxiety about their own monarch.[39] Analogy thus joins patriotism and anti-Spanish feeling. However commercially or pragmatically motivated, Peele fashioned a play which appeals to many contemporary interests. *The Battle of Alcazar* also marks an important stage in a significant Elizabethan dramatic process: shaping a play from an historical narrative. To a large extent, Peele was on his own here. *Tamburlaine* and Greene's *James IV,* for example, romanticize their historical material, vaguely enough known as it might have been, but the Armada and the Lisbon expedition of 1589 and the legend of Thomas Stukeley all force Peele into closer contact with "what really happened." Other historically based plays (like *Gorboduc* or *The Misfortunes of Arthur*) may have contributed dramatic devices or short cuts, but their misty, legendary subject matter allowed the dramatist more scope, or permitted more vagueness, than Peele could afford. A modern reader has trouble understanding the adjective in "The Tragicall battell of Alcazar."[40] Peele used the word partly to emphasize his play's truth and partly to emphasize its goriness: "this true and tragicke warre . . . full of bloud and ruth" (49–50).

From this perspective, Peele's use of pageantry and his repeated invocation of revenge and Nemesis propose a view of history and of man's place in it. To control his subject matter, Peele resorts to set-piece scenes of rich, public, political moments—the many meetings among important dignitaries, for example—but he surrounds them with the irony of deceit and with references to supramundane forces seeking death, destruction, and blood. Consequently, we rarely believe that individuals control events. Even as the characters pursue various abstractions (revenge, fame, holy war), impersonal forces—articulated by the Presenter or Muly Mahamet—take control of the outcome. In other words, human identity matters less than hatred, revenge, war, and all the other vivid abstractions framing the play's action. Human identity is very fragile, perhaps even unimportant, in *The Battle of Alcazar.* From the start, we all know the outcome. As he dies, Stukeley acknowledges this foredooming: "from our Cradles we were marked all / And destinate to dye in Affric heere" (1363–64). Various human motives—and the play supplies them amply—all finally subserve one catastrophic end, an end the characters acknowledge fatalistically and the audience foreknows historically.

Pageantry, bombast, the Presenter, and the dumb shows are, therefore, aptly chosen dramatic means. Perhaps Peele had few artistic choices and limited artistic resources, but the play balances its material and its method rather well. A modern audience may find the result unappealing, or stiff, or untragic. The Elizabethan audience clearly had a very different response. A great actor and a rich, marvel-filled production probably helped make *The Battle of Alcazar* a success. The play also makes its own success through effective references to current political events, a raucous patriotism, and a dramaturgy nicely suited to its subject.

Chapter Six
Edward I: In Peace Triumphant, Fortunate in Wars

Alone among Peele's dramatic works, *Edward I* appeared in two Elizabethan printings, the quartos of 1593 and 1599. Copyright records suggest that in 1600 yet another printer considered issuing the play.[1] Theatrical accounts confirm the play's popularity: Philip Henslowe's *Diary* lists fourteen performances of *Longshanks,* the king's nickname and apparently Henslowe's term for *Edward I,* between 29 August 1595 and 9 July 1596. "Longeshankes seute"—presumably the "suit of glass" Edward wears in scene 3—was still important enough to mention in two inventories of 1598.[2] As printed, *Edward I* has enough flaws to make acting it impossible without some rearrangement, cutting, or rewriting.[3] The existence of a printed text did not harm the play's theatrical success: Henslowe earned very respectable sums from *Longshanks* in 1595–96.[4]

Precisely when *Edward I* was written or first produced remains unknown, as it does for so many of Peele's plays. A text was certainly finished by 8 October 1593, when Abel Jeffes entered it as his property in the Register of the Stationers' Company. The likeliest period of composition (mid-1590–1592) falls in a stretch of very lean years for London theater companies. Many took to the road or dissolved and reformed or disappeared completely.[5] During this chaotic period, plays may have been cut and rewritten for smaller casts, or some may even have been stolen from their rightful owners or become the property of a united company which later divided, with each new company claiming ownership of a given play. In the confusion, certain facts remain: alone among Peele's accepted plays, *Edward I*'s title page neither mentions a theater company nor claims that the play was "publicly acted"; a play called *Longshanks* earned the Admiral's Men good returns in 1595–96; *Edward I* appeared in two editions before 1600. Thus, it is possible, if unlikely, that a version reached print before it, or another, reached the stage.[6]

Critics have added many speculations to these facts. A popular suggestion has been that the printed play includes partial revision, either by Peele himself or by some anonymous hand.[7] One critic has suggested that *Edward I* represents a "bad quarto," constructed surreptitiously by individuals (perhaps actors) who had neither artistic nor commercial rights to the play.[8] Peele's signature on the last page—"Yours. By George Peele . . ."—must mean that his original script underlies at least some of the play. What (or how much) of the 1593 quarto he hoped to see performed as a single theatrical event we cannot know.

Multiplicity of Action

The play itself employs three basic plot elements, and the title page promotes each, some rather sensationally. The first is more or less accurate historical narrative which Peele has steeply compressed and rearranged: "The Famous Chronicle of king Edward . . . with his returne from the holy land"; a second group of materials derives from popular tales of Robin Hood: "Also the Life of Lleuellen rebell in Wales"; the third element is a completely unhistorical characterization of Queen Elinor as divinely judged murderess: "Lastly, the sinking of Queene Elinor, who sunck at Charingcrosse, and rose againe at Pottershith, now named Queenehith." Peele apparently sought to subordinate the second and third plot elements within a frame tracing Edward's glorious military triumphs over the Scots and Welsh.[9] Despite a rather confused text, this plan can be seen again and again. Scenes 1 through 5 embrace the first cycle of the plot.[10] Informed of Henry III's death, "Triumphant Edward" (103) returns from the Holy Land to be crowned and to advance English domination over the British Isles. The Queen Mother, by way of prologue, offers praise of "Illustrious Champions" who have awed "neighbor realmes" (lines 11ff.). Edward rewards his loyal soldiers and urges his queen and chief courtiers to do the same (lines 118–80), but his daughter Joan (or "Jone")[11] worries about her mother's pride:

> Let not your honour make your manners change,
>
> . . . .

> That Prince were better live a private life,
> Then rule with tirannie and discontent. (246, 254–55)

Here, Joan both warns the Queen and praises her father. Throughout the play, Peele will contrast Edward with friends and enemies to create the image of a model king.[12] After this first contrast between Edward and Elinor, Peele introduces "Lluellen, alias Prince of Wales." Like the Queen Mother and welcoming English lords of scene 1, Lluellen also awaits a loved one, Elinor de Montfort, his English fiancée, who will help advance his political aims (lines 288–95). A group of comic characters—a Friar, his novice, his "wench," and a Welsh prophetic bard—appear. Incognito, Prince Lluellen cheerfully taunts his subjects until the Friar proves too good a cudgel-man and the Prince is forced to become friends with this ribald crew. Comic byplay ends abruptly when Lluellen learns that Edward has intercepted Elinor de Montfort's fleet. Open rebellion must follow: "To armes true Britaines sprong of Trojans seede, / And with your swordes write in the booke of Time" (610–11).

Contrasted with this Celtic rebellion is the loyal Scottish attitude of scene 3. Edward here resolves a dispute over who should rule Scotland. Following the English "Coronations due sollemnitie" (634), Edward chooses John Balliol as the true monarch of Scotland (lines 666–87). Like scene 1, this scene ends with an episode which juxtaposes Elinor's love for her husband (in a passage called "Queene Elinors speeche," lines 704–24) with her proud contempt for his subjects. When Queen Elinor meets the Lady Mayoress of London returning from her son's christening, she darkly threatens the poor woman, who can only wail, "Alas I am undone, it is the Queene, / The proudest Queene that ever England knew" (765–66).

In scene 4, Lluellen and his brother Sir David of Brecknock devise a plan to exchange David, a double agent whom Edward trusts, for the captured Elinor de Montfort, and the next scene shows the scheme's success. Edward releases Elinor and accepts an anonymous soldier's proposal for renewed peace and "A truce with honourable conditions"—"That none be Cambrias prince to governe us, / But he that is a Welshman borne in Wales" (996, 988–89). Only one character is displeased. Mortimer, earl of March, has fallen in love with Elinor, now Lluellen's bride (lines 1008–10). This scene ends the first cycle of the play's action, but several sources of future conflict have been introduced: Queen Elinor's pride, Mortimer's disappointed love, and the possibility of a new Welsh or, by analogy, Scottish rebellion.

As history has it, so the play: Edward immediately sets about meeting the Welsh demand for a native prince by summoning his pregnant queen to Wales. She understands his plan: "So then it is king Edwards pollicie, / To have his sonne, forsooth sonne if it be, / A Welshman" (1095–97). When the King and Queen meet in Wales, Elinor greets her husband angrily and strikes him (lines 1131ff.). This strange and unprovoked anger, so similar to her earlier outbursts, is excused as sickness and justified by Edward as a husband's proper humility (lines 1137–38). Even as Edward plans to circumvent the Welsh demands, Lluellen, his newly regained love, and their supporters decide—rather unexpectedly—to imitate Robin Hood. They will rove the mountain of Mannock Denny disguised as an outlaw crew, "men at armes and knights adventurous" (1217). Scenes 7 and 8 establish their comic masquerade and reveal Mortimer disguising himself as a potter to be near his beloved Elinor.[13]

Amidst this humorous and romantic disguising, a brief scene (9) reveals new political dangers: John Balliol has decided that "Scotland disdaines to carrie Englands yoke" (1413) and orders a courtier loyal to Edward: "Beare thou defiaunce proudly to thy king" (1421). As if in compensation for this new revolt, the future Edward II is born and declared "Edward of Carnarvan . . . And Prince of Wales" (1512–13). The scene of Edward II's birth also includes the happy portent of a marriage agreement between Joan and the earl of Gloucester, a union Elinor promoted and Edward heartily approves. Elinor herself, at first loving and tender, becomes suddenly vicious and requires her husband to order that all Englishmen's beards be shaven and that all Englishwomen cut off their right breasts. This sadistic demand, a new and more horrible example of Elinor's willfulness, is turned aside when Edward declares he will be the first shaven man and his wife the first mutilated woman: "Princes ought no other doe, / Faire ladie, then they would be done unto" (1676–77).

Scene 11 concludes the second cycle of action by showing Edward himself as a disguised member of Lluellen's band of outlaws. Edward and Mortimer eventually battle Lluellen and David. Each leader discovers that a trusted member of his entourage is in fact a traitor: "what Davy is it possible thou shouldest be false to England?" (1887)

and "no Potter I, but Mortimer . . . whose comming . . . is to deceive thee" (1893–94). At this point, both Welsh prince and Scottish king have revealed their enmity. Like the political order, Edward's family life, seemingly so happy and hopeful, will soon break down as well.

A cheerful, ceremonial scene (12) marking Prince Edward's christening and Joan's wedding is interrupted by news of the Scottish revolt, and Edward directs his forces against the two new threats:

> While wee with Edmund, Gloster, and the rest,
> With speedie journeis gather up our forces,
> And beat these braving Scots from Englands bounds,
> Mortimor thou shalt take the route in taske,
> That revell here and spoile faire Cambria. . . . (2011–15)

After a glimpse of Balliol's cruelty to Edward's messenger (scene 13), a truncated and incomplete scene shows Mortimer pursuing the Welsh rebels. Havoc and cruelty also move from Edward's realm into his family. Queen Elinor pursues the Lady Mayoress, whose earlier joy had so offended her. With grotesque cruelty, the Queen invites the Mayoress to become the nurse of young Prince Edward and orders a servant, Katherine, to

> binde her in the chaire,
> And let me see how sheele become a Nurse,
> So now Katherin draw forth her brest
> And let the Serpent sucke his fil, why so
> Now shee is a Nurse, sucke on sweet Babe. (2092–96)

Edward's successful Scottish campaign and Mortimer's defeat and beheading of Lluellen now appear in a series of short scenes (16, 17, 19). Interspersed with this reestablished political order are two scenes (18, 20) showing Queen Elinor's spectacular punishment. Thunder and lightning greet the Queen and her daughter on Charing Green. When Joan accuses her mother of murdering the Mayoress, Queen Elinor swears an unfortunate oath:

> Gape earth and swallow me, and let my soule
> Sincke downe to Hell if I were Autor of

> That womans Tragedy, Oh Jone, helpe Jone
> Thy mother sinckes. (2196–99)

No less spectacularly, the earth releases her (scene 20) amidst some splendidly blasé rural folk:

> *Potters wife.* . . . but staie John, whats that riseth out of the ground? Jesus blesse us John, look how it riseth higher and higher.
>
> *John.* By my troth mistres, tis a woman, good Lord do women grow, I never saw none grow before.
>
> *Potters wife.* Hold thy tongue, thou foolish knave, it is the spirite of some woman.
>
> *Queene.* Ha let me see, where am I, on Charing green? I on Charing greene here hard by Westminster, where I was crowned and Edward there made King, I tis true so it is, and therefore Edward kisse not me unlesse you will straight perfume your lips Edward.
>
> *Potters wife.* *Ora pro nobis,* John, I praie fall to your prayers, for my life it is the Queene that chafes thus, who suncke this daie on Charing greene, and now is risen up on Potters Hive, and therefore trulie John ile goe to her. (2266–81)

King Edward harangues the defeated Balliol in the short scene (19) between Elinor's sinking and rising. When Edward begins: "Now trothles King what fruites have braving boastes, / What end hath Treason but a soddaine fall?" (2208–9), it is hard to miss the parallel between political and moral "treason," between public and private rebellion against the king's peace. Balliol and Elinor both "fall."

Edward soon learns of his wife's "strange affright" (2330). Discovering that she has called for "secret conference with some Friers of France" (2332), Edward decides that he and his brother Edmund, duke of Lancaster, should "take the swete confession of my Nell, / We will have French enough to parlee with the Queene" (2334–35). At first, Edmund refuses to join this strange deception (lines 2337–45), but then reluctantly agrees. Scene 22 concludes the overt political plot of the play: the surviving Welsh rebels are dragged miserably toward London and execution.

Like the last act of *The Battle of Alcazar,* the final scene (23) of *Edward I* has suffered various unexplained textual indignities. If the opening stage direction is literally correct (*"Elinor in child-bed . . ."*), we may be meant to see the Queen returned once more to the point of her greatest happiness and the origin of her first violent anger toward the Lady Mayoress. Elinor's crime was a horrible parody of motherhood, and sexual crimes now fill her mind. Distraught and near death, Elinor wants to "repeat and so repent my sinnes" (2402). Edward and Edmund eventually arrive, *"in Friers weede,"* to hear Elinor confess "flocking troupes of sinne" (2447). She stuns her husband and brother-in-law:

> In pride of youth when I was yong and faire,
> And gracious in the king of Englands sight,
> The daie before that night his Highnes should,
> Possesse the pleasure of my wedlockes bed,
> Caitife accursed monster as I was,
> His brother Edmund beautifull and young,
> Uppon my bridall couch by my concent,
> Enjoied the flowre and favour of my love.
> And I becam a Traitresse to my Lord. (2469–77)

According to Elinor, "unto this sinne a worser doth succeede,"

> For Jone of Acon the supposed child,
> And daughter of my Lord the English King,
> Is baselie borne begotten of a Frier. . . . (2492–94)

Thus, Edward's "onelie true and lawfull sonne . . . his sonne that should succeed, / Is Edward of Carnarvan latelie borne" (2496–98). Her sins confessed, the Queen dies, and Edward orders Edmund away, promising, "Traitor thy head shal raunsome my disgrace" (2541). The King must now tell Joan of her mother's confession. Their meeting is poignant and painful for both ignorant child and too-knowing father. Elinor's adultery mortally wounds her daughter, and Joan first *"fals groveling on the ground"* and then *"dies at the Queenes beds feete."* Unfortunately, the text now becomes very confused and Edward is summoned offstage to deal with the Scottish and Welsh rebels we have already seen defeated.[14] Gloucester remains to lament his wife's death and is curiously interrupted by a silent *"Mortimor with the head"* (of Lluellen). Again, some textual confusion here gives the play a very lame and incoherent conclusion.

Extensive textual confusion appears before the play's finale. The 1593 quarto and the 1599 reprint have many signs of incomplete revision or rewriting. For example, Edward's seeming friend Sir David of Brecknock, Lluellen's brother, reveals his true allegiance in scene 11: "Edward I am true to Wales, and so have beene frendes since my birth" (1888–89). It comes as a surprise, therefore, to hear Edward say in the next scene, "Sir David you may commaund al ample welcome in our court, for your cuntreymen . . ." (1958–59). King Edward's enemies seem to possess miraculous powers of renewal, even resurrection. Lluellen, decapitated in scene 16, and Balliol, defeated in scene 19, both reappear as fresh threats in scene 23. There are many more inconsistencies and oversights.

Public and Private Life

Despite the textual confusion, we can detect a pattern designed to show Edward as a great English hero and model king who valiantly subdues his foreign and domestic enemies. To produce this clarity and symmetry, Peele has manipulated his historical sources very cleverly. Although Edward's tomb in Westminster Abbey calls him "Hammer of the Scots," he never lived to subjugate them entirely. At his death, his early Welsh campaigns—and his system of defensive castles which remain today—must have seemed a mockery of his later military failures. Peele has radically compressed and rearranged events to make the Welsh and Scottish rebellions coincide and to make Edward the undisputed victor in each. Time schemes and documented personal relations are juggled for most of the central characters: Queen Elinor died and her husband both remarried and died many years before Joan's death; although Joan reluctantly married Gloucester, she survived him and remarried. The contention for the Scottish throne among Balliol and eight other claimants actually postdates Elinor's and Lluellen's deaths by six years.[15]

Dramatic condensing of events and careers gives the opening five scenes their concise and sturdy structure. That group of scenes supports the many subsequent contrasts between Edward and his opponents. Peele develops this pattern in two directions, the public (Lluellen, David, Balliol) and the private (Elinor, Edmund, Joan). Although the lines probably belong elsewhere, Edward's final speech links these public and private threats:

> How one affliction cals another over.
> First death torments me, then I feele disgrace,
> Again Lluellen he rebels in Wales,
> And false Balioll meanes to brave me to,
> But I will finde provision for them all,
> My constancie shall conquer death and shame. . . . (2655–60)

Joan's and Edward's warnings to Queen Elinor (lines 246–55 and 1674–77, respectively) harp upon her responsibilities as both a private person and a queen. Elinor's personal crimes have, as we will see, very serious consequences for the royal succession not only in Edward's time, but in Elizabeth's, too. Other challenges to Edward's reign appear in personal terms: the traitorous Sir David is a trusted friend, the rebellious Balliol received his crown at Edward's hands. Mortimer and later Edward must disguise themselves in order to pursue personal aims (Mortimer's love for Elinor de Montfort) and public ones (Edward's suppression of Lluellen's outlawry), respectively.

Although Irving Ribner called *Edward I* "one of the crudest of the early English history plays,"[16] the public-private split has many dramatic advantages and also allows a good deal of covert political commentary. Shakespeare's English history plays often contrast a political figure's personal desires with his public responsibilities, and Marlowe uses the dichotomy very effectively in *Edward II*, a play written at precisely the same period as *Edward I*.[17] Given Peele's characteristic nationalism, his hatred of Spain and of Roman Catholicism, his version of Edward's career naturally promotes a strong central monarchy in recalling the Barons' Wars (lines 290–92), in condemning Welsh and Scottish factionalism, and in ridiculing Catholic piety through the licentious (and very amusing) Friar David. Edward meets the various threats, of course, as both a public and a private individual.

Contemporary Political Issues

Peele's introduction of Robin Hood has been condemned as a corruption of true dramatic history,[18] but the episode has both political and theatrical value. Temporarily defeated as a political force, Lluellen and his crew adopt the entertaining fiction of "Robin Hood and little John, / The Frier and the good Maide marrian"

(1521–22). Edward's reaction to their outlawry shows how different the Welsh imitators are from their originals. Masquerading as Robin Hood, Lluellen pursues his rebellious plans; unlike his legendary model, Lluellen does not benefit his society, nor can the forces of order accept him. The popular poem called *The Mery Geste of Robyn Hood* (London, ca. 1560) contains the most comprehensive known version of the Robin Hood saga and shows a king (identified as "Edward") disguising himself in order to meet and befriend Robin Hood; an identical episode (although the king is Richard the Lion-hearted) appears in Anthony Munday's play *The Downfall of Robert Earle of Huntingdon afterward called Robin Hood* (licensed for performance in March 1598 and printed in 1601).[19] Peele works against the tradition, then, when his disguised king fights the rebel disguised as Robin Hood. Like their illustrious popular models, they meet as private men rather than as king and subject, but the new masquerade fails just as open revolt had done. Tradition cannot make them friends and allies. Robin Hood legends were very popular and appear often in sixteenth-century ballads and plays, but pure entertainment cannot fully explain Peele's choice. By attaching the Robin Hood charade to Prince Lluellen, Peele assures that it will have a political valance: in Elizabeth's world, as in Edward's, independent armed groups were intolerable, no matter how charmingly decorated or seemingly innocent.

Peele has also been criticized for his completely unhistorical vilification of Queen Elinor. His chronicle sources portrayed her very differently, but here—as perhaps in the Robin Hood material—contemporary Elizabethan political issues have influenced the play. *The Battle of Alcazar* and *Anglorum Feriae* show how sensitively Peele responded to one of the major domestic problems of the 1580s and 1590s: who should or would succeed Queen Elizabeth? Marie Axton has recently recalled that one group of political writers answered this question with a candidate who must have horrified the nationalistic Peele: Isabella, the Spanish Infanta. From at least 1571, arguments favoring the Spanish claim had been put forward; in 1594–95 the pseudonymous R. Doleman (in fact the Jesuit Robert Parsons and other writers) published *A Conference about the Next Succession to the Crowne of Ingland.* This book earnestly discussed and seemed to approve the Infanta's rights, and plays like *Edward I* or *The Battle of Alcazar* or Robert Greene's *Friar Bacon and Friar Bungay* (which also concerns Edward and Elinor) can be seen as responses to such views.[20] Edward's queen formed part of the pro-Spanish argument, as did Edmund Crouchback, King Edward's brother and founder of the house of Lancaster. An artist who opposed that argument might rewrite history to poison the Spanish claim at its roots. Thus, Marie Axton holds that Peele "draws the portrait of a lustful fourteenth-century Spanish princess whose shameless incontinence before and after her marriage to Edward I leaves the entire genealogy (by which the sixteenth-century Infanta claimed) illegitimate. . . . Peele . . . asks the audience . . . to recognize the one sound branch of legitimate succession which will pass precariously through the weak Edward II."[21]

Peele stones two sinners, Elinor and her supposed paramour, Edmund, duke of Lancaster, because the Lancastrian line (through John of Gaunt) leads to the royal houses of both Portugal and Spain, including the late-sixteenth-century Infanta. Thus, Elinor conveniently confesses not only marital infidelity, but treason: she is a "Traitresse" (2477) and Edmund a "Traitor" (2541). That political interpretation of a private deed then extends forward in time to destroy the sixteenth-century Spanish claim. Should that claim still seem valid, Peele reminds his modern audience of their present monarch's "familiar majestie" (250) and the certainty of a foreigner's "Spanish yoake" (257). This argument and the related ones concerning the Robin Hood episodes or *The Battle of Alcazar* are of course not aesthetic or theatrical ones. Political convictions can neither explain nor justify Peele's dramatic success or failure. Fortunately, *Edward I* conveys its political and "Elizabethan" arguments rather well.

Edward's kingship and its public and private demands frame the entire action. Lluellen's masquerade as Robin Hood has a political motivation and continues his political conflict with Edward. The other large subsidiary set of events—Queen Elinor's crimes and their punishment—has political implications and, of course, affects Edward as an individual father and husband. Whether giving a close-up image of Edward as a loving husband or offering high-flown praise of his glorious English attributes, Peele generally concentrates on the public-private contrasts and on every action's political significance. A line from *Descensus Astraeae* might apply to Edward as well as to Elizabeth: "In peace triumphant, fortunate in wars."[22] The difficulties of triumph and victory form the play's substance.

Violence and History

A comparison of *Edward I* with *The Battle of Alcazar* identifies the history play's many unusual features. Peele's sources for *Alcazar* offered, if anything, too little action, while the chronicles of Edward's reign brimmed with complex events and manifold dangers. Indeed, Peele adds to the sheer amount of material his play must organize. *The Battle of Alcazar* seems to be a "tragedy" in Peele's view, however odd that designation may seem today, but *Edward I* did not need, in Elizabethan terms, to fit any precise generic formula. Although Peele has very skillfully rearranged his historical sources, his play need not provide any more causal explanation than the implied one: this event followed that event in history. He does provide a frame, of course, but it embraces more ample and varied actions than does *The Battle of Alcazar.* While *Alcazar* seems to take, at most, a few weeks, *Edward I* covers years. Variety of action produced greater variety in language and in social classes, but both plays regard their political and military subject matters as intensely violent.

Alcazar's violence, of course, resides largely in the language and in the dumb shows. We see Stukeley's murder and the quiet death of Abdelmelec, but the slaughter of Sebastian's army and their Moorish enemies, and the deaths of Sebastian himself and of Muly Mahamet, are presented either in hasty battle scenes or reported by others. *Edward I* is very different. To win Elinor de Montfort's release, Lluellen tortures his brother Sir David in full view of his English friends. According to the stage directions, David is stabbed *"into the armes and shoulders,"* threatened with *"hote Pinsers,"* and finally has his nose slashed. The sadism becomes all the more remarkable when we recall that Sir David agreed to be tortured and thus help Lluellen win back his love. When Balliol decides to throw off English domination, he sends Lord Versses *"with a halter about his necke"* as a messenger (scene 12). Edward replaces the halter with his "chaine" (1986, 1999), a ceremonial golden badge of rank (see line 2064), and tells Versses to "carrie" Balliol "this token that thou sendst" (2000). The symbolic exchange so enrages Balliol—"darst thou bring a halter to thy King?" (2061)—that he immediately orders Versses hanged on "a silver Gibbet . . . for fowles to feede uppon" (2065–66). Elinor, of course, progresses from the threatened mutilation of all the women in England to the torture of the Lady Mayoress, left to die in full view of the audience. During the Welsh battles, successive rebels appear preparing to commit suicide, and Lluellen is first *"slaine with a Pike staffe"* and then beheaded. Our last glimpse of the Welsh rebels is of Sir David *"drawne on a hurdle,"* a sledge for the public humiliation of condemned traitors,[23] and of *"Lluellens head on a speare"* (scene 22).

Although Marlowe has a modern reputation for staging violence, *Edward I* exceeds in variety and number the scenes of torture and cruelty shown in Marlowe's plays. Part of the explanation lies, no doubt, in the audience's taste; after all, they liked Marlowe's violence and Shakespeare's. Peele's contemporary concerns also made degrading Queen Elinor important. Significantly, Edward is insulated from the violence: he suffers its effects, but never instigates it. His only acts of physical violence are sword play (scene 11) and warfare (scene 19), acceptable and "heroic" deeds very unlike the torture and petulant cruelty of his enemies and betrayers. Finally, the staged violence vividly portrays the dangers of political action, specifically rebellion against legitimate authority. That is, the play's violent episodes manifest Peele's authoritarianism and its obverse, his anxiety about social instability.

Language and Characters

Violence is never far away in *Edward I,* and it appears at every social level in the remarkably diversified cast of characters. Quite unlike *The Battle of Alcazar* or any other of Peele's plays, *Edward I* embraces social groups from royalty and aristocracy through the middle class (the Lady Mayoress) to farmers and skilled laborers. Peele exploits the Welsh scenes and the Robin Hood episode to bring in "Morgain Pigot, our good welsh prophet" (469), with his doggerel songs, as well as a farmer-victim of Friar David's con game (lines 1734ff.), and Friar David's own entourage of Jack, a novice, and Guenthian, his "wholsome Welsh wench" (365). When the Queen rises from the earth at Potter's Hithe, two concisely developed local characters forget their own comic argument to greet the royal apparition. Aristocratic characters in the play can be appropriately dignified (in scenes like the welcoming of Edward, or his choice among the Scottish claimants to the throne) or properly classical in their allusions (like Lluellen worrying about Elinor de Montfort's safety or seeing her in Edward's custody). Peele also presents these public figures' human qualities sympathetically (the sweating, slippered queen of lines 1016ff., for instance, or Edward commiserating with Gloucester at lines 2620ff.).

The history play's loose definition freed Peele to imagine a wide range of social types. So freed, he created distinctive languages for those different characters and used as many poetic meters as he had done in *The Araygnement of Paris*. Royalty and aristocratic characters usually employ iambic pentameter, but conversations will sometimes become iambic pentameter couplets. Fourteeners appear rarely, often as a way of pointing a warning or drawing a slightly aphoristic conclusion. The scenes of Robin Hood and the scene at Potter's Hithe are principally in prose, with irregular four-stress lines for some of the songs. Aristocratic characters get drawn into prose when they converse with comic or rural or lower-class prose-speakers, but rarefied allusions and diction remain an upper-class prerogative. Some of the repetitions of Pigot's prophecies recall the similar repetitions in *The Old Wives Tale,* and Peele will typically have serious characters repeat each other's words at moments of crisis.

Whatever the dramatic forces shaping Queen Elinor's fictional personality, her speech has more variety than any other principal character's. She can be homely and downright, or angry and shrewish, or conscience-stricken, or loving. The remains of a fine speech can be detected in a confused passage when she rejects Joan's consolation (lines 2417–31), but an earlier speech is a tour de force. To celebrate Edward's coronation, Elinor demands that he "weare a sute that shee shall give thy grace, / Of her owne cost and workmanship" (217–18). This gift proves to be the "sute of Glasse"—apparently a garment decorated with numerous globes—which the impresario Philip Henslowe recorded in his inventory of 1598. Gazing at her husband, Elinor delivers a complex speech which even has its own heading, *"Queene Elinors speeche"*:

> The welken spangled through with goulden spots,
> Reflects no finer in a frostie night,
> Then lovely Longshankes in his Elinors eye:
> So Ned thy Nell in every part of thee,
> Thy person's garded with a troope of Queenes,
> And every Queene as brave as Elinor,
> Gives glorie to these glorious christall quarries,
> Where every orbe an object entertaines,

> Of riche device and princelie majestie.
> Thus like Narcissus diving in the deepe,
> I die in honour and in Englands armes:
> And if I drowne, it is in my delight,
> Whose companie is cheefest life in death,
> From foorth whose currall lips I suck the sweete,
> Wherewith are daintie Cupids caudles made,
> Then live or die brave Ned, or sinke or swim,
> An earthlie blisse it is to looke on him.
> On thee sweete Ned, it shall become thy Nell,
> Bounteous to be unto the beauteous,
> Ore prie the palmes sweete fountaines of my blisse,
> And I will stand on tiptoe for a kisse. (704–24)

Frank Hook complains that this speech is "so extravagant that it verges at times on nonsense,"[24] but the dramatic situation justifies the extravagance and "nonsense" is unfair. The Queen's verbal play turns upon ideas of reflection: the image of what we see reflected in our eyes ("lovely Longshankes in his Elinors eye") and the image of herself reflected in the numerous glistening orbs of Edward's suit ("thy Nell in every part of thee"). Reflected images of the Queen—"riche device and princelie majestie"—"gard" (decorate, protect) the King. The glass seems a pool in which Elinor sees herself reflected, Narcissus-like, and may even drown, but living or dying is all the same so long as she has Edward's love. His beauty, enriched by all the reflected images of his queen, excuses her forwardness: "On thee sweete Ned, it shall become thy Nell, / Bounteous to be unto the beauteous," and the complicated puns of the final couplet ask for a kiss. "Ore prie" means "overpeer," that is, "excel" and "look over"; palm trees were a conventional Renaissance emblem of married happiness. The "fountaines" of Elinor's "blisse" are Edward's eyes, reflecting her image, her eyes reflecting his image, the "glorious christall quarries" of his suit, and finally the pool wherein Narcissus drowned himself in love.[25] Edward Longshanks was extremely tall and could therefore "look over" a queen who has to "stand on tiptoe for a kisse." Physically and emotionally, Edward overpeers or excels conventional wedded happiness when he kisses his wife. Although the mythologizing, the opulent language, and the complicated figurative thought all make the speech very formal and courtly, the use of nicknames, the homely image of a night sky, and the proverbial phrase ("or sinke or swim") also make it warmly intimate.

Peele may have added this speech when revising the play.[26] Whether or not a late addition, the speech collects some important ideas and presents them very theatrically. Elinor's deep love and Edward's response are etched in the speech. Later he will say, almost unwillingly, "Fast to those lookes are all my fancies tide [tied]" (1629). The speech also hints at the dangers of Elinor's own pride: Narcissus is an ambivalent mythological model. Theatrically, Peele establishes the richness of scene, costumes, and court, and Edward's most notable physical quality, his great height. Finally, the speech images a happy and secure peace—wedded love, the coronation, and the end of Scottish discord—which will be first disturbed and then destroyed in coming scenes.

Edward I has many verbal styles besides the one in Elinor's speech; the play ranges more widely than any other Peele wrote. Most notable here—and it can be found elsewhere in the play—is the way even a very formal speech also possesses dramatic value. We admire the language, the allusions, the complicated puns, but we also recognize that this speech will lose important qualities when removed from its dramatic context. Nor is that context only the immediate one: the speech summarizes what goes before and anchors what follows it. This is language written for stage delivery, and Peele shows here and elsewhere in the play his sense of drama as well as his lyric gifts.

Theatricalism

All the verbal artistry of Elinor's speech depends, of course, on a single spectacular fact: Edward's costume. Only if we imagine (or see) this remarkable glass suit can we wholly appreciate Peele's lyric skill. Lyric and dramatic cannot be separated. While the suit has a bizarre fascination, the quarto allows us to deduce much more about how the play might have appeared. Paradoxically, the text's uncertain auspices make it an intriguing source of information about staging.[27] However close or distant Peele's connection with the printed text (and his signature means he cannot be too far behind at least some parts), the stage directions often provide a powerful impression of a play on the stage. For example, the processional stage direction (after line 40) mentions *"every man with his red Crosse on his coate.*" These red crosses are not just decorative or historical detail. Peele clearly has them in mind when Rice ap Meredith sadistically suggests that Lluellen "sacrifice" David of Brecknock in Elinor's presence "which beeing done, one of your souldiers may dip his foule shirt in his bloud, so shall you bee waited with as may crosses as king Edward" (944–47).

Even more interesting are stage directions which seem to describe an actual performance, or an imagined one firmly based in practical experience: for example, the directions after lines 1015, 1453, 1932, and 1940. These directions resemble those in *The Old Wives Tale* and *David and Bethsabe.* Like them, they imply simultaneous staging; several imaginary locales coexist on the stage. They further suggest that the Admiral's Men must have provided some fairly substantial props, like Elinor's "litter." It might be possible for Queen Elinor to display her infant son in an alcove or curtained doorway at the rear of the stage, but references to a "Tent" suggest a fabricated playing-space like King David's tent in *David and Bethsabe.* Directions often refer to geographical locales as if they had recognizable embodiments on stage:

Exeunt ambo from Wales. (after line 2175)

The Frier having song [sung] *his farewell to his Pikestaffe a* [he] *takes his leave of Cambria, and Exit the Frier.* (after line 2146)

Peele, or whoever wrote these directions, may have let his imagination run free, but the implication—again—is that the audience had some tangible reason to associate a place name with a certain structure on the stage, or a specific area on the stage.

Finally, some of the stage directions already mentioned and others make the text sound like that of *The Araygnement of Paris;* it becomes almost a production record meant to be read, like those we associate with masques. For example, the stage direction which ends "*Bishop speakes to her in her bed*" (after line 1940) is centered above the Bishop's speech, which lacks a separate speech prefix, and the same thing occurs after line 1964: ". . . *Longshanks speaketh.* / What tidings bringes Versses to our court?" Earlier, when Edward has persuaded Elinor not to pursue her vicious attack on English men and women, he rebukes her, "Leave these ungentle thoughts, put on a milder mind . . ." (1681). She replies angrily, dismissing him, and "*The*

Nurse closeth the Tent" (after line 1686). The 1593 quarto then prints a quotation from Horace, italicized and centered in the middle of the page:

Quo semel est imbuta recens servabit odorem Testa diu

(The jar will long keep the fragrance of what it was once steeped in when new)[28]

This classical observation sounds like an author's comment to a reader, since the next speech has its own prefix and concerns (appropriately in the dramatic context) Elinor's Spanish pride and her insulting behavior to the King.

Masquerade and Politics

Just as uncertainties about the text qualify our conclusions on how the Admiral's Men might have staged *Edward I,* so too textual muddle prevents dogmatizing about the play's literary or aesthetic values. After all, the 1593 quarto may include an anonymous reviser's work, and it certainly has some inconsistencies which neither Peele nor a theater company would be likely to approve. Nonetheless, we may admire Peele's artful handling of his historical sources, the way political issues link the Robin Hood and the Queen Elinor episodes to the historical action, the play's wide range of verbal styles, and the diversity of the characters who use them.

One other motif repays attention. When Shakespeare and Marlowe dramatize the conflict between a politician's public and private selves, their plays often become studies of deception and role-playing. Thus, for example, Prince Hal declares he will pretend to be worse than he is in order to appear still better when he publicly renounces his old ways. On other occasions, a political design or disaster will force a public character into some unwanted deceit. At one such moment, Marlowe's Edward II and Peele's Edward I speak the same line: "Hence faigned weedes unfaigned is my griefe" (2519, and see *Edward II,* 4.6.96, substituting "woes" for "griefe"). Edward Longshanks's disguise as a French friar is only one among many disguises—conscious and unconscious, literal and figurative—in the play. As a rebel prince, Lluellen appears physically disguised from the very start (scene 2) and eventually leads his entire entourage into the Greenwood fantasy. Mortimer disguises himself for love,

Sir David of Brecknock for political advantage. Physical conflict and political crisis finally force both men to declare their true allegiances (scene 12). John Balliol appears a loyal dependent until he abruptly declares his true hatred (scene 9). In Peele's rewritten history, Elinor and Edmund disguise their moral natures until Edward's physical and spiritual disguising uncovers their guilt. Joan, of course, discovers that her status—royal princess and wife of Gloucester—is a fraud, and the discovery kills her. Indeed, deception revealed almost always causes violence, and the revelation often requires violence. Queen Elinor's attempt to deny murdering the Lady Mayoress leads to the most spectacular "revelation," the supernatural sinking and rising.

Disguise, masquerade, and deception are, in fact, endemic. The characters' announced or implied motives range from romance and lust to consolation, self-protection, and patriotism; consequences include comic entertainment, theater spectacle, and disillusionment. Amidst this variety, the pattern remains constant, too constant for chance, although the textual confusion prevents any unequivocal judgment about Peele's artistic design. Yet, Werner Senn has shown conclusively that Peele almost always uses repetition for emphasis and structure. Within *Edward I*'s slightly random action, multiple disguises do point out parallels and, sometimes, ironic contrasts. Does Peele use these episodes as more than a device to highlight and organize small units of his play? Part of the answer lies in what the play's disguises do not do. They do not serve conventional romantic or comic ends, as they do in Robert Greene's nearly contemporaneous *James IV* and *Friar Bacon and Friar Bungay*. Mortimer does not win the lovely Elinor de Montfort, for example, and Peele inverts the age-old story of the husband who poses as his wife's confessor.[29] In Peele's version, the deception produces unhappiness rather than comic embarrassment and reconciliation.

Although disguise does not serve traditional comic purposes, it does inevitably accompany political action. Edward finds again and again that political motives conceal or distort the true face of friends (Sir David), allies (John Balliol), and even wife and brother. In *The Battle of Alcazar,* we recall, Stukeley accuses Philip of "disguising with a double face" (808), and King Sebastian's other ally, Muly Mahamet the Moor, proves equally deceitful. Since Peele never uses disguise elsewhere—if we except the magical transformations of *The Old Wives Tale*—its concentrated presence in *Edward I* and the figurative mention in *The Battle of Alcazar* plausibly suggest that he regarded deceit, masquerade, and disguise as facts of political life. At the same time, however, disguise does not satisfactorily advance any political cause in *Edward I,* as it sometimes does in Shakespeare's history plays. Instead, violence almost always trails disguise, and deception leads to death.

Disguise does more than underline local parallels, then, but it hardly creates an overall dramatic statement. Indeed, for a modern taste, *Edward I* may try to encompass too much. Almost every separate element—the historical action, the Robin Hood and comic episodes, the love of Edward and Elinor, as well as the Queen's crimes and the diversified groups of characters, for example—is well and attractively developed. The play's contemporary success, in fact, suggests that modern critics decry precisely the qualities that pleased Elizabethans most. Neither Elizabethan generic conventions nor the public theater audience demanded intensity or concentration in a chronicle history play. If anything, the genre's loose definition and the audience's appetite for variety invited a rambling, excitement-filled production. Peele's play answers these implicit demands quite skillfully.

As the extensive, ahistorical revision of Elinor's life shows, *Edward I* also draws contemporary Elizabethan concerns parallel with historical or pseudohistorical events. Even without the succession issue, the play offers a grim account of political life. Violence, deceit, and a wearying course of troubles crowd the play. Although Edward himself appears a model king and model Englishman, his every success introduces a new challenge, despite Peele's careful selection and rearrangement of historical fact. Even the amusing comedy of Friar David and his fellows concludes with political defeat and death; Joan and Gloucester's marriage has been made unhistorically happy in order—it seems—to intensify their pathetic end. Peele's good theatrical sense accounts for this variety: the play includes something for everyone. His own political and social interests contribute a tone and presentation which are at once monarchist and insecure. Consequently, what might almost be nostalgia for the days of "Triumphant Edward" and "Illustrious England" coexists with pervasive violence and public chaos.

Chapter Seven

David and Bethsabe: The Tower and the Lute

In writing *The Love of King David and Fair Bethsabe. With the Tragedie of Absalon,* the best surviving late-Elizabethan play on a biblical subject, Peele exploited one of the finest texts in all Scripture.[1] William F. Stingspring describes the Second Book of Samuel as having "such remarkable historical and literary quality that its author deserves the title 'the father of history'—a title usually given to the Greek historian Herodotus, who lived five hundred years later."[2] The biblical author cares most about Israel's political and religious fate and the relation of her early kings, especially David, to God and His divine program. The writer moves with telling simplicity through the familiar story of David's lust for Bethsabe, his removal of her husband, Urias, and the birth of their legitimate son, Salomon. Woven into this basic story are various episodes—Ammon's rape of his half-sister, Thamar; Absalon's revenge for this violation; Absalon's rebellion against his father, David; and later his own death—which amplify David's troubles and represent the "consequences" of his adulterous love.[3] Peele concentrates on David's reign and ends his play with the promise of Salomon's kingship, but he often rearranges, condenses, or omits biblical material to suit his own personal and typically Elizabethan interests.

The Opening of the Play

In the opening of *David and Bethsabe* many remarkable features prove Peele's lyric gifts and illustrate his skillful control over dramatic design, a talent critics have often denied he had.[4] An actor speaks the prologue and then becomes a "presenter" when he *"drawes a curtaine, and discovers* [reveals] *Bethsabe . . . bathing over a spring."* We immediately recognize a kinetic union between the actor who introduces us to Peele's verse and the dramatized figure who introduces the action. The actor takes an intermediate position between the audience and the play, bridging the imaginative space between the theater audience and the play's fictional world.

"Of Israels sweetest singer now I sing," the Prologue begins, echoing both 2 Samuel 23 and the invocation of classical epic. Peele personalizes the play and advances himself and his poetic task: "I prease [strive, come forward] to sing" (Prol., 15). This quality continues through an extended comparison between the Prologue and David, the ancient and revered singer of psalms to God. The poet-Prologue cannot hope to match a man "Whose Muse was dipt in that inspiring deaw, / Arch-angels stilled from the breath of Jove" (Prol., 3–4). While David's sacred music drew heavenly beings down to earth (Prol., 8, 12–13), the poet-Prologue sets himself a different, more secular task: "helpe devine Adonay to conduct, / Upon the wings of my well tempered verse, / The hearers minds above the towers of Heaven" (Prol., 16–18). That is, God ("Adonay") must help Peele's earthly Muse raise the audience's minds up to heaven, even as David's song once brought heaven to earth. Alas, the poet uses an "yron Pen" (Prol., 23), while David's "consecrated fingers strooke / The golden wiers of his ravishing harpe" (Prol., 9–10).

This self-criticism helps avert a charge that Peele is blaspheming or committing sacrilege in undertaking a biblical fable about a king who became a "type," or allegorical anticipation, of Christ.[5] Similarly, the smooth mingling of biblical and pagan terms (Adonay and Jove, for example, or the entire classical machinery of Muse and invocation) keeps Peele's artistic enterprise from approaching too near the sacred. In the end, Peele very tentatively associates himself with David and seeks both the assistance and the protection this great "original" poet offers his successor.

A movement of ascent and descent controls the Prologue, but when the presenter reveals Bethsabe and we hear her song, a new pattern appears. Her beautiful lyric employs oxymorons—"Hot sunne, coole fire . . . Blacke shade, fair nurse"—to ask protection from the sun and seek the tempering of "sweete aire." The verse shifts from iambic pentameter to trimeter for an ominous final stanza, and the trimeter itself breaks down in the last couplet:

> Let not my beauties fire,
> Enflame unstaied desire,

Nor pierce any bright eye,
That wandreth lightly. (30–33)

Suddenly, the sun's heat, from which Bethsabe is shrouded, becomes transformed into beauty's fire, rays which can and do enflame desire: David soon describes "all mine eyes with all thy beuties pierst" (130). After her song, Bethsabe calls upon "Zephire . . . and thy sister, soft and sacred aire, / Goddesse of life, and governesse of health" (34, 41–42) to "stroke my bosome" because the winds can enter the shade which is "sun proofe." Bethsabe's rich language emphasizes the sensuous, almost unearthly quality of her beauty and her pleasure in it. At the same time, her fears of being seen and of arousing "unstaied desire" appear in the pattern of force and obstacle which controls her description of the sun's forbidden presence, the shade's shrouding, and the wind's insinuating entrance. Bethsabe's bower protects her from the sun's heat and allows the soothing winds to reach her, but it neither prevents David's eyes from being "pierst" by her beauty nor keeps the "wind" of her song, her words, from piercing David's soul, "incensed with a suddain fire" (50).

Thus the play's opening establishes two patterns, one vertical (the ascent to heaven, the descent to earth; the relation of God and man) and the other horizontal, a pattern of penetration and resistance appropriate to the sensual and earthly seduction about to occur. These two patterns continue throughout the play and even seem to control some of the stage action (the ascent to the tower of Rabba, for example, or David's falling to the stage where he hears Nathan's prophecy). Peele has invented these patterns. His biblical source, 2 Samuel 11:2–4, is very brief and direct. Both Peele and the Bible, of course, emphasize David's illicit watching, but Peele's dramatized version uses the poet-Prologue and the audience's normal relation with theater-spectacle to associate us with David. The King watches the beautiful bather in much the same way (and presumably with many of the same thoughts) as members of the audience.

The Prologue and first scene of *David and Bethsabe* introduce many patterns of action, many stage images, many figures of speech and allusions which will be repeated or echoed and amplified through the remainder of the play. Among the many notable features of the play's beginning, four stand out: allusion to Adam and Eve; the mingling of pagan and Christian material; a logical pattern based upon the four elements; the importance of the King's private actions to his nation's welfare.

When David first sees and hears Bethsabe, he searches for the most intense and significant comparison to express his wonder:

> What tree, what shade, what spring, what paradise
> Enjoyes the beautie of so faire a dame?
> Faire Eva plac'd in perfect happinesse,
> Lending her praise-notes to the liberall heavens,
> Strooke with the accents of Arch-angels tunes,
> Wrought not more pleasure to her husbands thoughts,
> Then this faire womans words and notes to mine. (51–57)

"Paradise" perhaps suggested the comparison with Eve, but it is an ominous one. Eve's words and looks eventually affected Adam's thoughts in ways mankind regretted; David and Bethsabe will repeat that pattern. Cusay shortly urges Bethsabe that "The King . . . hath liberall hands" (98), and the phrase more than casually echoes "liberall heavens" because the liberal hand soon violates the edict of the liberal heaven, bringing anguish and suffering to the lovers and their country. When David imagines Bethsabe's approach (in language recalling Canticles 2:8–9), he promises

> To joy her love Ile build a kingly bower,
> Seated in hearing of a hundred streames,
> That for their homage to her sovereine joies,
> Shall as the serpents fold into their nests,
> In oblique turnings wind their nimble waves,
> About the circles of her curious walkes. . . . (117–22)

"To joy" means "to enjoy." The phrase compactly says, "to gain her love," "to satisfy her love," and "to take [my] pleasure in her love." More disturbingly, the water/serpent image recalls the "waveless spring" (38) Bethsabe leaves and the snake in man's first garden.

David's opening speech to Bethsabe quietly alludes to a pagan mythological incident which will return several times in the play:

> As heavens bright eye burnes most when most he climes
> The crooked Zodiake with his fierie sphere,
> And shineth furthest from this earthly globe:

> So since thy beautie scorcht my conquerd soule,
> I cald thee neerer for my neerer cure. (131–35)

The imagery of sun far and near recalls the episode of Phaethon (a son as beloved of Phoebus as Absalon is of David) and his disastrous steering of the sun's chariot too close to the earth. Punning on "neerer" (closer and sooner), Peele emphasizes that Bethsabe's approach further inflames David and brings adultery closer to fulfillment. Like Phaethon, Absalon will be inflamed to replace his father, and like the mythological figure, the biblical son will cause earthly suffering and his own death. Peele carefully ascribes fiery qualities to Absalon, who claims his rebellion will make "heaven . . . burne in love with Absalon" (1118). Again, Peele mixes biblical with pagan allusions to deepen and amplify as well as decorate his subject.

Another pattern, this one physiological in origin, runs through the play's opening lines. Bethsabe's song and initial speech touch on fire, air, and water, three of the four elements which, for an Elizabethan, composed all created things, animate and inanimate. By easy assimilation, these elements were concorded with the four "humors" whose balances and imbalances determine the human psychological makeup. Thus, David's striking locution completes the quartet of elements even as it illustrates his lust's release:

> Bright Bethsabe gives earth to my desires,
> Verdure to earth, and to that verdure flowers,
> To flowers, sweet Odors, and to Odors wings,
> That carrie pleasures to the hearts of Kings. (90–93)

This speech brilliantly employs the rhetorical figure called "climax" or "*gradatio*," in which a word that ends one clause is repeated at the beginning of the next. In the second line, the dramatist turns the figure inside-out: earth/verdure/earth/verdure, but then it proceeds regularly: flowers/flowers/odors/odors/wings. Instead of repeating "wings," Peele then releases the pent-up energy created through repetition in the (literally) soaring, longer final clause. The King has forgotten his rational and spiritual allegiances and submits instead to his concupiscence: his earthly desires fasten upon Bethsabe, their incarnation. It is a familiar, though unusually well-turned, Elizabethan imagining of lust's dominion.

David's adulterous design cannot escape God's notice or his retribution. Indeed, the play's opening brims with explicit and implicit acknowledgments of God's special interest in Israel and his stern demands upon those who profess belief. The Prologue, of course, calls upon Adonay, David soon mentions Aaron (71), the first anointed priest, and Cusay assures Bethsabe that David is "Elected to the heart of Israels God" (103). This last fact, David's election or special choosing as leader of Judah and Israel and the first good king after the warfare and suffering of Saul's kingship, made his religious responsibilities coterminous with his political ones. Such a link between principal worshiper and principal magistrate would naturally be congenial to an Elizabethan audience accustomed to regarding their monarch as "God's lieutenant" and head of the Church of England. Responding to Bethsabe's fears (line 108: "I hate incontinence"), Cusay announces an important and damaging corollary: "Woman thou wrongst the King, and doubtst his honour, / Whose truth mainteines the crowne of Israel" (109–10). David's "truth," his faith, and spiritial purity alone sustain the political entity he had done so much to shape. If his private moral behavior weakens, it is not only a personal failing; it threatens the survival of the chosen people themselves. Peele consequently organizes much of the play through linking the monarch's own spiritual and psychological condition with the health or illness of his nation. David's responsibilities are not public or private as different cases may be: everything he does and everything he is constitute his people's fate. The play's title and the prologue pinpoint the two chief public-private facts of David's life: *The Love of . . . Fair Bethsabe. With the Tragedie of Absalon.*

Royal Adultery and Royal Authority

By an abrupt transition typical of Peele's dramaturgy in this play, the second scene shifts us from the King's private immorality to the main political and military threat Israel faces: the Ammonites. From luxury, sensuality, and softness, we move suddenly to: "Courage ye mightie men of Israel, / And charge your fatall instruments of war / Upon the bosomes of prowd Ammons sonnes" (157–59). Joab's loud vaunt—"Ye fight the holy battels of Jehova" (163)—stresses anew the way Israel's success and future rest on her citizens' faith.

The shift to military action emphasizes the public context of David's adultery, but only because Peele has rearranged his biblical material.[6] He takes some details from 2 Samuel 10 and combines them with details from 2 Samuel 12. In effect, this order reverses the Bible's chronology. The scene also recalls the opening very effectively. First when Urias, Bethsabe's husband, counsels his leaders to "assault and scale this kingly Tower, / Where all their conduits and their fountaines are" (180–81), he almost certainly indicates the same part of the stage (perhaps a free-standing prop, perhaps part of the theater structure) David occupied when he first observed Bethsabe. Cusay then told her, "the King of Israell / From forth his Princely tower hath seen thee" (94–95). When David finally conquers Rabba, he specifically mentions "Rabbaes raced [razed] towers" (816). Eventually, Peele fuses the moral and political-military significance of "tower" in David's lament:

> Ah Absalon the wrath of heaven inflames
> Thy scorched bosome with ambitious heat,
> And Sathan sets thee on a lustie tower,
> Shewing thy thoughts the pride of Israel. . . . (986–89)

Identifying the physical location of David's sinful act with the location of his first major military victory allows Peele to associate that sin with Israel's further political problems. As David recognizes, Absalon's revolt punishes his father's adultery, and son follows father into a figurative "tower of lust."

With the adulterous affair established and its potential political effects hinted, Peele's next scene introduces his third important and related interest, David's "beauteous son," Absalon. Again, Peele reorders the biblical account and approaches Absalon obliquely through the story of Ammon's incestuous rape of Thamar, Absalon's full sister and Ammon's half-sister. As David had claimed to be when he saw Bethsabe, so Ammon claims he is "amorously leane" (255; compare lines 135–52). Jonadab acts as pimp, and while Thamar trustingly seeks to heal her brother's "crased [crazed, diseased] soule" (280), the pander muses:

> Why should a Prince, whose power may command,
> Obey the rebell passions of his love,
> When they contend but gainst his conscience,
> And may be governd or supprest by will. (282–85)

Why indeed? Jonadab's soliloquy makes plain the parallel of lust and political unrest through the familiar Elizabethan equation of man's physical microcosm and the social macrocosm. Like David, Ammon has put his passions, not his reason, in command. The consequences will be terrible for Thamar, for Ammon, for Absalon, and for David himself. Jonadab's speech continues almost as a report of the rape and its sequel (lines 286–306). Emphatic repetition of "Now" (286, 289, 296) gives the speech the immediacy of a continuous description of the rape. Organic images—Ammon's "withered cheekes" (288), Thamar's "ripened . . . holy fruits" which "grew" and then became "rotten"—aid this sense of a speech recording not a static situation, but an action which continues even as the speaker speaks. Finally, the "dishonour" that hunts Thamar "through every covert shade" uncovering "shame and nakednesse" (296–98) recalls the shade that could not protect Bethsabe from David's lust.

The play's dramatized action resumes at a point perhaps halfway through the narrative we have just heard, for Ammon enters *"thrusting out Thamar."* Curiously, she claims "The banefull torment of my publisht shame" is a "second evill" which "far exceeds the first" of the rape itself (312, 315). Only when we realize that the published shame, the known dishonor which Jonadab had also emphasized, spreads the evil deed to the commonwealth, the state of Israel itself, can we understand Thamar's torment. These wrongs done by and to the King's children will not only destroy the royal family (Absalon, after all, immediately vows revenge), they will also disgrace the ruler. Like David's own lust, this rape will threaten the nation's very existence. Thamar laments that she has been "cast as was Eva from that glorious soile . . . To desart woods, and hils with lightening scorcht" (322, 326), and her words remind us that David compared his love with Eve emparadised. When Thamar tells Absalon what has happened, his curse distills the implications of Thamar's "Tragicke spoile": Ammon is "Traitor to Heaven, traitor to Davids throne, / Traitor to Absolon and Israel" (349–50). Once David learns of the rape, he recognizes his own responsibility (lines 384–85). The sinful tyrant (line 391) is none other than David himself.

According to 2 Samuel 13:23, "two yeres" pass between the rape and its revenge, but Peele again rearranges the biblical account. He steeply compresses its time scheme to dramatize the endemic corruption David's sin has brought his family and nation. Absalon at once offers an ominous invitation: David and "all his other lords," including Ammon, must come "Up to my sheepe feast on the plaine of Hazor" (397–98). Before we see Ammon's murder amidst this ceremonial social occasion, however, we have seen another deliberately fradulent social occasion, itself created and defiled to advance sin and death. Hoping to "save" Bethsabe's "renowne" and legitimize her pregnancy, David urges Urias to "take thy rest, / Visit thy wife and houshold" (447–48). When further urging fails, David dupes Urias into drunkenness, again through exploiting his servant's loyalty and the social occasion (repeated toasts to Joab, to David, and to David's children). The ironies are strong: even in drink (itself a sin), Urias refuses to betray what he deems his trust; moreover, the deceitful toasts prove their own undoing since the health of David's children (Ammon, Absalon, and the unnamed child of adultery) will soon fail utterly. David resolves to place Urias in the most dangerous part of the battlefield and thereby rid himself of an obstinately loyal and foolishly trusting servant.

Here ends the first movement of Peele's play. The Chorus appears to reprehend David and to narrate undramatized events: Urias's death and the birth of the King's illegitimate child (lines 552–74). This first section of the play has established the origin of David's problems, his unrestrained passions, and pursued the consequences of that error in Ammon's rape and Absalon's plan for revenge. The second section takes up these matters principally in David's relation with his supposed successors, either Ammon or, failing him, Absalon. David's royal weaknesses encourage Absalon's attempt to usurp the throne. In this long middle section we also find David attempting to rectify his personal sins and his political mistakes. These efforts lead not only to sorrow and humility, but finally to the event that promises so much for Israel's future, Salomon's appearance and nomination as David's successor. Throughout the play's opening, Peele introduces certain motifs—the imagery of fire, the spatial image of the tower, and the significance of David's psalmistry—which form a graceful but sturdy link among his main dramatic concerns.

Retribution for Urias's murder (or virtual murder) comes quickly: Bethsabe enters, mourning her child's illness ("sicke, sicke to death"). David the psalmist cannot cure her unhappiness with music (lines 580–83) because he is responsible for it; furthermore, the sin that created the child taints his relation with God, formerly expressed through joyous songs of praise. As with Thamar's violation, the special punishment here lies in publicity: "For who is it among the sonnes of men, / That sayth not . . . the King hath sind" (591–92). Bethsabe resolves "in humblenesse" to await "The grace that God will to his handmaid send" (600–601).

Just as David's music could not console his lover, so he too wishes to "dash" his "yvorie Lute against the stones" (605) in token of his grief and sin. Nathan comes to his king with the familiar parable of the poor man from whom his little was taken while the rich man saves his much. "What," the prophet asks, "shall be done to him for this?" (629). David judges fairly, but thereby condemns himself. Nathan promises, "from this day forth, / The sword shall never goe from thee and thine" (647–48). David abases himself, but Nathan raises him up, promising that the Lord "hath seene / The true repentant sorrow of thy heart"; nonetheless, "The child shall surely die, that erst was borne, / His mothers sin, his kingly fathers scorne" (661–62; 668–69). In a symmetrical, ten-line speech ending with almost the same couplet, David accepts God's judgment and welcomes the favor which spares the true criminal, the King himself. Cusay enters immediately to announce that the child has died. In another of the abrupt emotional changes typical of the play and of Peele's conception of David's personality and history, the King proclaims: "The child is dead, then ceaseth Davids shame" (696). David's repentance and the child's death have purged his private sin. Music and praise of the Lord are once more possible (lines 699–703), and we watch a courtly interlude of music, song, feasting, and perhaps even dance. This ceremony, unlike the murderous feast at Hazor or the drinking bout with Urias, properly and appropriately celebrates a personal and, tentatively, a national purification. At once, the newly invigorated king sets out to finish the conquest of Rabba.

In the imaginary time David takes to reach and attack the city, we watch the fatal revenge upon Ammon, accompanied by a mock ceremony of dancing and singing shepherds. Knowing that Jonadab even now carries the news of Ammon's death, we cannot share David's great and devout joy at Rabba's capture. Wearing Hannon's crown, he proclaims, "The God of Syon and Jerusalem . . . hath exhalted Israel to this" (822–23). Again, Peele has reordered the biblical account to interrupt triumph with defeat: "how soone are

Davids triumphs dasht, / How suddenly declineth Davids pride" (846–47). No sooner has God's punishment and forgiveness restored David's ability to rejoice in music, song, and victory than once more he plunges into loss:

> Ammon thy life was pleasing to thy Lord,
> As to mine eares the Musike of my Lute,
> Or songs that David tuneth to his Harpe,
> And Absalon hath tane from me away
> The gladnesse of my sad distressed soule. (875–79)

This equation of sons with song will prove most important at the end of the play, but the pattern of alternating elevation and descent appears again here. It continues in the next two episodes: first, through Joab's efforts, the "widdow of Thecoa" employs a parable to reconcile David to Absalon, and then Absalon immediately decides to replace his father. Thus, in a very brief space (approximately 630 lines, or about the length of a long Shakespearean act), David has moved from the despair of his interview with Nathan, to the joy of his renewed allegiance to the Lord, to victory over Rabba, to sorrow at Ammon's death, to reconciliation with his son's murderer, and then to the threat of Absalon's revolt.

These alternations are not chance, nor are they biblical. The author of the second Book of Samuel tends to pursue each narrative element to its end before taking up another strand. Peele has interwoven these episodes, even rearranging and condensing the biblical chronology, to produce extraordinary swings of emotion and spirit. Similar abrupt transitions occur earlier and later in the play. Other patterns, too, echo this one—the ascent/descent pattern of the Prologue, for example, or the vivid contrasting stage pictures of royal towers and collapsed, huddled figures.

Clearly, this pattern is deliberate and imposed. It reflects Peele's interpretation of David's relation with "Jacob's God" and the effects of his subtly but swiftly changing human psychology. Partly, no doubt, David's historic importance to Israel and the nation's precarious existence make the pattern plausible. Nor would a late-Elizabethan audience be immune to fears for national survival and especially for the royal succession. By choice or happy chance, Peele expresses David's character in his fortune's violent changes; at the same time, he portrays a pressing current preoccupation of his audience. Moreover, the play has made an important step beyond most serious contemporary drama because it now achieves an ironic, albeit external, vision of the central figure. The audience no longer skips willy-nilly and perpetually surprised from incident to incident. Instead, we view successive triumphs or defeats with increasingly complex emotions. In one sense, we—like David—begin to understand the enormous promise and demand his anointment carries.

The Central Scene

Rapid transitions from joy to sorrow and back again lead us to the play's literal and figurative center. Just halfway through the play occurs a most curious scene (lines 973–1106), virtually a council of war among David and his remaining supporters. During the undramatized interval between Absalon's resolution to usurp his father and this scene, Absalon has rallied many followers at Hebron (see 2 Samuel 15:9–13). David flees Jerusalem and takes refuge on "this holy Mount . . . this mount of Olives" (1004, 1006).

At first glance, the scene on the Mount of Olives appears no more than a versification of 2 Samuel 15, replete with David's sorrow and some complicated but dull political debates and decisions. Neither sorrow nor debate is insignificant. David despairingly recognizes his own responsibility: "Proud lust the bloudiest traitor to our soules, / . . . Thou art the cause these torments sucke my bloud" (973, 976). As their king has done, David's followers fall to the ground and lament their outcast state, but Sadoc, "high priest, preserver of the arke / Whose sacred vertue keepes the chosen crowne" (1021–22), encourages the King:

> . . . mourne not as a faithlesse man would doe,
> But be assurd, that Jacobs righteous God,
> That promist never to forsake your throne,
> Will still be just and pure in his vowes. (1017–20)

This speech is central to the play's vision of its subject, for David's despair effectively blasphemes against God's word. Unless he can overcome his entirely human and understandable grief at Absalon's defection (lines 1025–27), David cannot achieve what the Lord commands, nor can he truly have faith. While Sadoc might be expected to speak as he does, David's next comforter surprises the King. Ithay, "sonne to Achis mightie king of Gath" (1041), counsels strength and a counterattack. David cannot understand: "But wherefore goest thou to the wars with us? / Thou art a stranger here in Israel" (1039–40). Ithay sturdily declares he will remain "As sure as Israels God gives David life" (1048). The oath tells all. Ithay, a Gittite and a foreigner like the loyal Urias, teaches the anointed King what it is to have faith.

Each dialogue in the scene turns on issues of loyalty and disloyalty, faith and doubt, truth and falsehood. David decides to continue the struggle "with an humble heart" (1063) and dispatches Sadoc, Ahimaas, and Jonathan to Jerusalem, there to learn what they can. Ithay announces the unpleasant news that Achitophel, David's "auncient counsellor," has deserted to Absalon. Achitophel's intelligence makes him a formidable adversary. As if to forestall new despair, the loyal Cusay enters, and David decides to send him—as a false "traitor"—to Absalon in the hope that "Achitophels counsell may be brought to naught" (1099). Sadoc and Abiathar will act as spies, sending messages via Ahimaas and Jonathan. Thus once more, and this time for good, David has been taught both humility and faith. Surrounded by the confident priest, the stunningly loyal foreigner, and the devoted follower (Cusay) who will pretend to betray his king in order to annul the counsel of a real traitor, David at last commits himself to the God who is "spotlesse in his vowes" (1023). Priest and layman, royal stranger and devoted fellow Israelite all join to teach David the truth of his anointment and the splendor of his mission.[7]

David and Absalon

Reversing the biblical chronology, Peele follows this important scene with the immediate political consequences of David's decision. A crowned Absalon appears, surrounded by others *"in great state,"* and asks, "What times and orders we may best observe, / For prosperous manage" of the imminent battle (1190–91). Achitophel's wise counsel fails, and Cusay's "treasonous" (actually pro-David) advice wins Absalon's consent. Cusay dispatches Ahimaas and Jonathan to tell David the reassuring news. Before those messengers arrive, however, we see Semei's public attack on David. By reversing the biblical sequence, Peele ensures that this scene demonstrates David's humility rather than his humiliation. Confident that David's military enemies have made an inescapable tactical blunder, we accept his serene humility (lines 1322–25) as both just and justified. Our confidence is satisfied when the messengers arrive from Jerusalem and David orders his troops to battle. His final speech demands that his army "spare the young man Absalon" and recalls, ironically as events prove, that "Joab . . . didst once use friendly words / To reconcile my heart incenst to him" (1396–98). David must still discover that his sin's consequences will require further sacrifice.

Peele reminds us, through Achitophel's entrance *"with a halter"* and his preparation for suicide, that Absalon has made a poor military decision. Further, Absalon acknowledges that his own death is "Joves just doome" (1438). The moral, political, and emotional frame for Absalon's death is now almost complete. Hard on the heels of his rejected counselor, Absalon enters to deliver an important (but nonbiblical) speech encouraging *"his traine"* of supporters. This speech completes Peele's preparation for the second major climax of the play: Absalon appropriates some familiar biblical language describing God's love for Israel, and he once more adopts his own personal imagery of fire, light, and sun. Absalon claims "God in the whissing of a pleasant wind, / Shall march upon the tops of Mulberie trees" (1455–56) as a sign of his favor and approval, but the image recalls two biblical passages specifically describing God's military assistance to David in his anti-Philistine campaigns (1 Chronicles 14:15 and 2 Samuel 5:23–24).

The image portends Absalon's defeat and clearly reveals the struggle as one for God's favor rather than a mere political conflict between father and son. Absalon prays:

> Now Jove let forth the golden firmament,
> And looke on him with all thy fierie eyes,
> Which thou hast made to give their glories light,
> To shew thou lovest the vertue of thy hand,
> Let fall a wreath of starres upon my head,
> Whose influence may governe Israel,
> With state exceeding all her other Kings. (1443–49)

Absalon simply regards himself as God's noblest work, the source of the firmament's glory, or its purpose; he calls down the stars to give him astrological "influence" (a distinctly Elizabethan touch) over Israel. Absalon plans that his face will "shine in honour brighter then the sunne" (1451). The figurative language recalls Absalon's earlier vaunts, when he claimed "heaven shall burne in love with Absalon, / Whose beautie will . . . cloth the suns spheare with a triple fire" (1118–20), and we may well remember David's description of the fiery "wrath of heaven" which will punish his son's disobedience (986–89). Again, the mythological example of Phaethon looms dangerously close.

Omitting all but the most abstract evidence of battle (the stage direction says merely, *"The battel"*), Peele moves directly from this staggering boast to its pitiful conclusion, Absalon's celebrated entrapment in a tree and his execution by Joab. The entire scene concludes the terrible events David's adultery began, or so Peele's design would have us believe. Great and effective ironies suffuse the scene. Absalon's beautiful hair, for so long his pride and most persuasive attribute, now becomes "this unpleasant curle" (1474); the man who believed himself the "choisest fruit of Natures workemanship" hangs "like a rotten branch" (1477–78). Absalon desperately cries for a pagan, not a Hebrew, miracle: "let my beautie fill these sencelesse plants, / With sence and power to lose me from this plague" (1482–83). Ovid could do no less. Finding his king's enemy helpless, Joab taunts Absalon: "Now Absalon how doth the Lord regard / The beautie whereupon thy hope was built" (1517–18).

Joab's speech is Peele's own creation. It declares that Absalon is "Rebell to nature, hate to heaven and earth" (1511) for his revolt against David, Israel, and the Lord's decree. Begging for his life, Absalon despairingly wishes that David's "melting eyes / Might pierce this thicket to behold thy sonne" (1533–34). He thus recalls his death's origin, for David's eyes all too easily pierced the "bushly thicket" (45) protecting Bethsabe's nakedness. Thus began the sinful chain of events which Absalon used to justify his rebellion and which his death must finally expiate. An anonymous soldier enters to bury the body "in some ditch amids this darksome wood" (1559) and contemptuously asks, "Where is the vertue of thy beautie Absalon, / Will any of us here now feare thy lookes?" (1551–52). "Virtue," which means both "moral good" and "power," succinctly sums up the scene's ironies and the entire course of Absalon's career and its relation to David's actions. The human response to beauty, the overconfidence great beauty confers, and the pride of self-love all coalesce to capture the wrong of both father and son. However David might lust after Bethsabe's beauty, or Absalon trust to his own,

"God affects not any painted shape" (1521). As the Chorus summarizes, God regards only "the vertue of an upright soule," not "fickle beautie" or "glorious shapes" (1577, 1576).[8]

The Poet-King

To prepare us for the very mixed emotional tone of the concluding scene, Joab delivers a nonbiblical speech reconciling the enemy army "To Israels weale, to David, and to heaven" (1608). He then dispatches messengers to inform David "of our good successe" (1630) and, of course, to tell him that his "deerest sonne" (1535) has died a usurper's death. When David enters, with Bethsabe, Nathan, and, for the first time in the play, Salomon, we do not have quite the abrupt emotional shift Peele's technique has led us to expect. Instead, David's "thoughts retaine a sad conceit" (1645) despite the fact that "every pleasure kneeles before his throne, / And sues for sweet acceptance with his grace" (1646–47). He and Bethsabe exchange an extraordinary pair of speeches in which David's lute gains all the attributes of pagan Orpheus's instrument (1648–52) and David imagines "Faire peace" and "the ancient golden world" in terms (1660–70) which would not disgrace a classical Greek poet or an imitating Renaissance one. To alleviate David's melancholy thoughts of Absalon, Bethsabe finally asks,

> . . . is the pleasure of my soveraignes heart,
> So wrapt within the bosome of that sonne,
> That Salomon, whom Israels God affects,
> And gave the name unto him for his love,
> Should be no salve to comfort Davids soule? (1673–77)

While the audience tensely awaits the announcement of Absalon's death, the still-anxious David asks his youngest son if he will "imbrace / Thy fathers precepts" and zealously practice "such sacred principles / As shall concerne the state of Israel" (1697–98, 1700–1701). Salomon's reply explodes—curiously, anachronistically, and wonderfully—with a typical Renaissance longing for power, for knowledge, for control. Only Dr. Faustus's dreams of the "world of profit and delight, / Of power, of honor, and omnipotence" which await the necromancer can match Salomon's words. David sternly warns his precocious son, "Wade not too farre my boy in waves too deepe" (1726). Chastened, Salomon promises to rise only "on the burning wings / Of zeale devine" and hold "his eyes fixt on Jehovaes browes" (1766–67, 1770). Adapting a passage from 1 Kings 1:28–30, David bestows Israel's crown on this young prince so clearly destined for Elizabethan as well as biblical greatness (lines 1776–78).

Only now, with the nation's fate secure and David reconciled with Bethsabe and Nathan, does Peele spring the emotional trap. Three characters enter in rapid succession: the first announces the arrival of news "forth the warres"; the second, Ahimaas, proclaims David "blest with victory"; the third and last declares that Absalon "Sustained the stroke of well deserved death" (1782, 1788, 1804). Any competent dramatist might have exploited the Bible's "two-messenger" hints, but the repeated blows of joy and sorrow are nonetheless effective. Heartbroken, David once more abandons his music, believing he has lost God's favor: "tosse my broken Lute to heaven, / Even to his hands that beats me with the strings, / To shew how sadly his poore sheepeheard sings" (1824–26). David's mournful retreat *"to his pavillion,"* where he *"sits close a while,"* clearly recalls his physical collapse in the climactic scene on Mount Olivet (lines 992ff.).

Nathan protests that his king and queen "offend the highest, / To mourne in this immeasurable sort" (1837–38), but it is Joab, the loyal murderer, who finally reconciles David to his son's death. Significantly—in view of Absalon's revolt and Salomon's promised reign—Joab emphasizes David's political responsibilities: David must preserve Israel (1859–69) and punish the wicked (1870–79). His final tactic is a threat: "I sweare, / Ile lead thine armies to another King, / Shall cheere them for their princely chivalrie" (1880–82). Joab's terms, "chivalrie" and later "Fame" (1889), complete the mantle of Renaissance heroics thrown over the play's final scene. The biblical Joab is much less eloquent and far more bluntly concerned with David's preservation: "Now therefore up, come out, and speake comfortably unto thy servants: for I sweare by the Lord, except thou come out, there wil not tary one man with thee this night: and that wil be worse unto thee, then all ye evil that fel on thee from thy youthe hetherto" (2 Samuel 19:7). Peele transforms David into a classical-Elizabethan ideal prince. Perhaps he goes too far: David's response to Joab sounds very like *Lycidas*'s conclusion.[9] The King imagines his beloved son "freed from the yoke of earthly toiles" (a nice reminiscence of Absalon's betraying hair). His son is now a "changed spirit" among angels and "Saints," his "eyes now no more eyes but shining stars" (1898, 1902, 1905, 1908). It is very nearly an aria and concludes with the most extraordinary Christian anachronism of all: "Thou shalt behold thy soveraigne face to face, / With wonder knit in triple unitie" (1914–15).

However roughly neglect, or the theater, or the printer may have treated the play we read, *David and Bethsabe* retains a convincing power, order, and beauty. Peele takes a typically Elizabethan angle on his material: the king's private immorality taints the nation and threatens its future, especially through endangering the royal succession. David's wavering faith, his spasms of lust and guilt, violation and repentance, all have national and political consequences. His "example" implicitly encourages Ammon and unleashes Absalon's revenge; his dereliction, in turn, ignites Absalon's ambition; his return to true faith secures both the present and the future. Throughout, Peele responds to the poet-king as both an admiring fellow poet and as an Elizabethan citizen aspiring to courtly favor. Thus, David's lute, his psalms, and an Orphic conception of poetry represent his emotional state. Peele also dramatizes the King's condition through effective stage pictures: David summoning Bethsabe "up" from her bathing; David cast down on Mount Olivet; David hiding from sorrow and his court when Absalon dies. Fire, light, and sun image both David's lust and his son's rebellious ambition. Just as David equated his son Ammon with his sacred music (875–79), the lute's "golden wiers" and the golden hairs of his "beauteous sonne" become one. David can sing only in praise and faith; God denies him any other use of his talent. So, too, the handsome son misuses his beauty, and God insures that the epitome of that beauty, Absalon's glorious hair, kills him.

Peele may have originally planned, as the second choric speech implies, to end the play with David's death. The present conclusion, however, does fulfill the Prologue's hope that the poet may lift "The hearers minds above the towers of Heaven" because both Salomon's ambitious desire for knowledge and David's vision of a heavenly Absalon do just that. Finally, we recall Bethsabe's speech on David's Orphic lute, which can

> . . . make the mountaines dance,
> Retrive the sunnes sphere, and restraine the clouds,
> Give eares to trees, make savage Lyons tame,

> Impose still silence to the loudest winds,
> And fill the fairest day with foulest stormes. . . . (1648–52)

These three speeches summarize both a religious fervor and a most secular one. Peele has created a play which satisfies his faith, his political anxieties, and most interestingly of all, the vibrant Renaissance literary desire to make poets, at long last, kings.

Chapter Eight
Primus Verborum Artifex

When Christ Church, Oxford, invited Peele to help entertain the Count Palatine in 1583, the college authorities acknowledged a reputation that must have grown very rapidly. A year later, *The Araygnement of Paris* reached print; as early as 1582, Peele had become sufficiently involved in the London literary scene to write a prefatory poem for Thomas Watson's *Hekatompathia.* Excerpts from Peele's works appear in such contemporary anthologies as *The Phoenix Nest* (1593), *Englands Parnassus,* and *Englands Helicon* (both 1600). References to his name and work exist from the late 1580s forward; the complimentary ones offer insights into his circle of friends, and the neutral or negative ones unexpectedly present him as something of an archetypal Elizabethan poet.

Contemporary Opinion

Thomas Nashe and Robert Greene were apparently well acquainted with their fellow university graduate. Nashe's vitriolic preface to Greene's *Menaphon* (1589) pauses in its condemnation of much sixteenth-century English writing to praise three "most able men to revive Poetry." With Matthew Roydon and Thomas Achlow (or Acheley), Nashe lists Peele and calls him "the chiefe supporter of pleasance now living, the *Atlas* of Poetrie, and *primus verborum Artifex:* whose first increase, the arraignement of *Paris,* might pleade to your opinions his pregnant dexterity of wit, and manifold varietie of invention; wherein *(me judice)* he goeth a steppe beyond all that write."[1] Nashe presumably singles out *The Araygnement* because he is contrasting English and Italian successes in "pastorall poems," but his discriminating comments elsewhere in the preface suggest that Nashe meant his praise seriously and that he chose "dexterity of wit, and manifold varietie of invention" thoughtfully. A few years later, Robert Greene addresses part of *Greenes Groats-worth of Wit* (1592) "To those Gentlemen his Quondam acquaintance, that spend their wits in making Plaies." Although Greene names none of these "Gentlemen," his descriptions of the "famous gracer of Tragedians," "young Juvenall, that byting Satyrist," and "thou no lesse deserving than the other two, in some things rarer, in nothing inferiour" are clear enough to identify Marlowe, Nashe, and Peele, respectively.[2] Greene's special and self-pitying interest is to attack the actors and persuade his friends that playwriting is a contemptible occupation, an "extreme shift" and "meane stay" unworthy of their talents. Despite the special pleading, Greene's mention of Peele in such company should probably be taken as an accurate contemporary estimate.

Marlowe, Nashe, Greene, and Peele apparently formed a literary "set" in the London of the 1580s and early 1590s.[3] As late as 1607, Thomas Dekker thought of them as a group. His *A Knights Conjuring* continues Nashe's *Pierce Penilesse His Supplication to the Divell* (1592). At the very end, Dekker imagines himself in the portion of the Elysian Fields reserved for poets, "The Grove of Bay Trees." Dekker describes "old *Chaucer* . . . circled a round with all the Makers or Poets of his time," *"Grave Spencer,"* "learned *Watson,* industrious *Kyd,* ingenious *Atchlow.*" Meanwhile, *"Marlow, Greene,* and *Peele* had got under the shades of a large *vyne,* laughing to see *Nash* . . . still haunted with the sharpe and *Satyricall spirit."*[4] Dekker quite naturally includes Nashe because his own text depends upon *Pierce Penniless,* but his mention of the other poets suggests that even many years after their deaths, the three were remembered as a group typifying high Elizabethan literature.

Several plays, all probably written about the turn of the century, satirize lines, characters, and situations from *The Battle of Alcazar.*[5] These allusions (in such plays as *2 Henry IV, Poetaster,* and *What You Will*) generally characterize a speaker as having old-fashioned literary taste. Peele would not have been worth satirizing if his plays could not plausibly represent an older literary generation and taste which self-consciously "new" writers like Jonson and Marston wished to supersede. Similarly, *The Merrie Conceited Jests of George Peele* (1607) suggests that, more than ten years after his death, Peele was remembered as a name associated with the vivid and thriving literary decades at the end of the sixteenth century. The jest book has little or no factual link with Peele, but the book-buying public was obviously expected to respond to his name.[6] Dekker's *A Knights Conjuring, The Merrie Conceited Jests,* and various satirical allusions all imply, then, that Peele had become an archetypal Elizabethan writer, hardly remembered in any detail but rather a useful figure on whom to hang attitudes pro and con about more recent literature.

Modern Criticism

Since the Renaissance, criticism has followed Nashe in part of his praise: most modern writers regard Peele's lyric gift as his principal achievement. F. P. Wilson, for example, describes Peele's contribution to Elizabethan dramatic language as "a melody more than ordinary," a use of Spenserian or Sidnean mellifluousness for dramatic purposes.[7] This melodic gift accounts for the steady series of selections from Peele's work published in the twentieth century.[8] Although *The Old Wives Tale* has been paid the compliment of at least two modern rewritings,[9] Nashe's remark about "varietie of invention" has become matter for modern complaint. Most critics, after praising Peele's lyricism, damn his ability at dramatic construction. Madeleine Doran, for example, castigates *Edward I* and *David and Bethsabe* for their "shapeless unselectivity of incident," and scores of voices agree with her.[10]

This attack usually settles on the pageantry and "shows" of Peele's plays as their abiding defect. G. K. Hunter draws a painful contrast: "Lyly's comedies never degenerate, as Nashe's and Peele's court plays do, into *shows*"; in *The Araygnement,* he finds that the play "emphasized the local effect at the expense of continuity, turning what might have been a play into a 'show.' "[11] Muriel Bradbrook extends the same attack to *The Old Wives Tale:* "there is no need for . . . orderly sequence of plot or dramatic connexion" because the characters have "no need to play an action: merely to display themselves for what they were."[12]

This view of Peele's plays (and it is a very general one) does not survive unscathed a rigorous formal analysis like that of Werner Senn, and Inga-Stina Ewbank has argued that spectacle and the spectacular in fact unify all of Peele's dramatic works.[13] Moreover, the execrated showlike qualities of Peele's plays often make effective drama. Dumb shows and the Presenter in *The Battle of Alcazar,* for example, manifest an important dynamic of the play's world, its fatalism and highly determined nature. When *David and Bethsabe* employs "shows" and other supposedly undramatic devices, the audience perceives the mystery and burden of kingship itself, as well as the equally mysterious nature of a divinely ordained magistrate. From his pageant-writing and his descriptions of Elizabethan court ceremonies, Peele learned the value of interposing a twilight figure between his audience and the play they watch. These figures—Madge in *The Old Wives Tale,* the Presenter in *Alcazar,* the Prologue and Chorus in *David and Bethsabe,* for instance—serve remarkably varied dramatic purposes, and they cannot be dismissed as damaging or inartistic remnants of Peele's work as a court and civic poet.

That work taught Peele what the public liked, and they evidently liked ceremonies, processions, and similar episodes. He often turns both experience and popular demand to dramatic advantage. These qualities also reveal the playwright's political and cultural concerns. Sometimes, static speeches and static ceremonial episodes invite the audience's iconographic interpretation: that is, they operate analogically. Thus, when King Sebastian delivers his awe-struck praise of Queen Elizabeth (*The Battle of Alcazar,* lines 688ff.), the speech becomes an alogical but powerful "argument" for Thomas Stukeley's decision not to attack England. Similarly, the highly patterned but initially disrupted shows and gift-giving ceremonies of *The Araygnement of Paris* become an ordered praise of, and admonition to, Queen Elizabeth and her government. At the same time, there often lingers a certain insecurity in Peele's plays. G. K. Hunter has shown that "Lyly's court comedies are not required to justify the activities they flatter,"[14] but *The Araygnement* does betray an author anxious to defend the social order he praises.

Elizabethan Politics and Peele's Plays

Anxiety about domestic instability and foreign threat appears very clearly in *Descensus Astraeae* and *Anglorum Feriae;* the same anxiety resurfaces in *Edward I* and *The Battle of Alcazar.* In those plays, the "shows"—especially royal and/or political ceremonies—might encourage a skeptical modern audience to think about duplicity. Public relations and political showmanship were no less a part of Elizabethan governance than of modern, as Peele's own efforts for the Accession Day Tilts reveal. Indeed, Peele's historically based plays use a lightly sketched irony to frame public and deceptive political occasions: the diplomatic meetings of *The Battle of Alcazar,* for example, or the pretended threat to the spy Sir David in *Edward I,* or the fradulent social ceremonies of *David and Bethsabe.* Moreover, the temporarily defeated Welsh characters of *Edward I* actually create a make-believe society, more or less as a refuge from political disappointment. In *The Battle of Alcazar,* Abdelmelec's corpse "set . . . in his chayre with cunning props" serves his nation's political purposes just as well as the "manly man" did alive. Peele develops this ceremonial and grotesque image from the merest hint in his source.[15]

The modern reader might deduce that Peele viewed man's social and political life—his "historical" life—as feigned. Just such inferences have been drawn from Shakespeare's history plays. While Peele invites these speculations, his plays do not fully support them. The contrasting, unfeigned or "private" life rarely develops as a norm to measure the deceptive public life, although the Ned and Nell episodes of *Edward I* provide some slight domestic contrast with the monarchs' public roles. Another qualification to this view is Peele's evident skill at creating spectacles for their theatrical effect alone.

Despite these qualifications, we can still recognize that Peele's plays often reveal fragile human identity, political chicanery, and private relations absorbed into large, often hostile, political events or historical forces. Even Peele's deliberate and historically false vilification of Queen Elinor shows how far political needs—in this case contemporary Elizabethan ones—could override both a clear dramatic characterization and the facts as Peele knew them. In this latter case, contemporary forces directly influenced the making of the play as well as the life represented within that fiction. Peele's own artistic acts become, therefore, further examples of the individual's subordination to public life and cultural values.

The Elizabethan Writer in Society

The place of Peele and Nashe or Greene or Marlowe in Elizabethan culture was paradoxical. They were both that culture's spokesmen and its victims. Depending upon the "meane stay" of the theater and reposing "eternitie in the mouth of a Player," they tried to defend poetry and to please a society which starved them.[16] The writer is on the one hand a social outcast or at least a marginal figure: poverty stricken, unsatisfied in terms of status, fame, and influence; on the other hand, he expresses or hopes to express the dominant cultural values and other ideas of his society. Instead of being wholly integrated into the culture whose values he espouses, or appears to espouse, he is often rejected or ignored by that society except as a means, a tool. Peele's literary energy—in *The Honour of the Garter* or *David and Bethsabe*—often arises from his attempt to overcome this profound split. Trying to reconcile his professional ambition with social facts that explicitly or implicitly deny that ambition, he produces some exciting work. In *Edward I* and *The Battle of Alcazar,* contemporary events permit the artist to submerge himself (and his professional problems) in the mass. He shares the crowd's values and therefore can become both a spokesman for the crowd and a member of it. Finally, a third combination of paradoxical elements appears when Peele attempts to mirror experiences he cannot in practice share, although he may admire them and recognize that they express values he does share. These occasions are of course courtly ones.

No individual can be fully conscious of the historical and social forces which shape his personality and his work. Yet the Elizabethan debate over the moral, aesthetic, and commercial value of writing made Peele and his fellows hypersensitive to the social role of poet and poetry. This study has tried to identify the ways Peele's art responds to his culture's political and social cruxes. One of those cruxes was writing itself, and Peele very occasionally makes poetry and the poet his subjects. In *The Honour of the Garter,* he calculatedly links heroism with patronage, and the collapse of patronage becomes a symbol of political decay. Both poetry and nation may be revived, but they go hand in hand. The singer-spokesman has momentarily made himself and his profession the song itself. Peele moves from the obvious political advantage of the Garter ceremony to make professional advantage for himself; if Elizabeth and her government can use art to achieve other ends, so can the artist. Perhaps the highest flight of Peele's poetic/political ambition appears in his last play, *David and Bethsabe.* The historical accident of a poet-king permitted him to write about both subjects in seeming to write about one.

By another historical accident whose irony Peele would be unlikely to appreciate, he came to represent his generation of late Elizabethan poets. For Dekker, he was one of the poets worth remembering and praising; for dramatists eager to replace him and his contemporaries, he became a figure to be mocked. Perhaps most remarkable of all is the speed with which Peele and his fellow University Wits were displaced.[17] Marlowe, Greene, Peele, and a few others had created much of the most memorable and accomplished literature in a period of burgeoning artistic achievement. Yet Peele's career lasted at most a decade and a half, and by 1600 virtually all his artistic associates were dead or pursuing interests far removed from literature. Brief and complicated as his career was and however pathetic his end, Peele does merit a place in "The Grove of Bay Trees." He is a thoroughly representative Elizabethan writer.

Notes and References

Sixteenth-century titles have been slightly modernized. "Yale ed." refers to Charles Tyler Prouty, gen. ed., *The Life and Works of George Peele,* 3 vols. (New Haven, 1952–1970).

Chapter One

1. British Library MS. Lansdowne 99, folio 151; see Yale ed., 1:105 and the reproduction on 1:106.
2. Yale ed., 1:108.
3. See Anthony Esler, *The Aspiring Mind of the Elizabethan Younger Generation* (Durham, N.C.: Duke University Press, 1966).
4. All the biographical fact in this chapter derives from the splendid "Life" of Peele by D. H. Horne in Yale ed., 1:3–146.
5. See Mark H. Curtis, *Oxford and Cambridge in Transition, 1558–1642* (Oxford: Clarendon Press, 1959): for the universities as "the chief gateway to preferment," see p. 74; for Oxford as a "finishing school" for certain classes of students, see Lawrence Stone, "The Size and Composition of the Oxford Student Body 1580–1910" in Lawrence Stone, ed., *The University in Society,* 2 vols. (Princeton: Princeton University Press, 1974), 1:9.
6. For competition in the political sphere alone, see Wallace MacCaffrey, "Place and Patronage in Elizabethan Politics" in S. T. Bindoff, Joel Hurstfield, and C. H. Williams, eds., *Elizabethan Government and Society* (London: Athlone Press, 1961), pp. 95–126.
7. Curtis, *Oxford and Cambridge in Transition,* p. 269.
8. The poem is reprinted, ibid., p. 270.
9. The quoted phrase is applied to Oxford by Stone in "Size and Composition of the Oxford Student Body," 1:29; for Cambridge, see David Cressy, *Literacy and the Social Order: Reading and Writing in Tudor and Stuart England* (Cambridge: Cambridge University Press, 1980), Table 7.7 and p. 169.
10. Quoted in Mark Curtis, "The Alienated Intellectuals of Early Stuart England," *Past and Present* 23 (1962):28. Note also his remarks on the high expectations of graduates (pp. 38–39).
11. Edwin H. Miller, *The Professional Writer in Elizabethan England* (Cambridge, Mass., 1959), p. 8; see also Phoebe Sheavyn, *The Literary*

Profession in the Elizabethan Age (Manchester, England, 1909), pp. 138–39 and Appendix.

12. G. K. Hunter, *John Lyly: The Humanist as Courtier* (London, 1962), Chapter 1.

13. R. W. Bond, ed., *The Complete Works of John Lyly,* 3 vols. (Oxford: Clarendon Press, 1902), 1:4.

14. Quoted in Stone, "Size and Composition of the Oxford Student Body," 1:29; for further evidence (ca. 1577) see William Harrison, *Description of England,* ed. F. J. Furnivall (London: New Shakespeare Society, 1877), Part 1, p. 77.

15. See John Danby, *Poets on Fortune's Hill* (1952; reprint ed., Port Washington, N.Y.: Kennikat, 1966), Prologue and Chapter 1, esp. pp. 16, 22, and 44–45; Patricia Thomson, "The Literature of Patronage, 1580–1630," *Essays in Criticism* 2 (1952):267–84, esp. 269–70 and 278; J. W. Saunders, *The Profession of English Letters* (London, 1964), Chapter 3. Although Peele knew Spenser's poetry well enough to borrow from it, their careers, if not their attitudes toward poetry, are very different. Peele wrote to live; Spenser managed the reverse. See Richard Helgerson, "The New Poet Presents Himself: Spenser and the Idea of a Literary Career," *PMLA* 93 (1978):893–911.

16. See Nashe, *Have With You to Saffron-Walden,* in Ronald B. McKerrow, ed., *The Works of Thomas Nashe,* rev. ed., F. P. Wilson, 5 vols. (Oxford: Blackwell, 1958), 3:30–31.

17. Cf. Yale ed., 1:56 and 1:80 (on *A Tale of Troy*), and Werner Senn, *Studies in the Dramatic Construction of Robert Greene and George Peele* (Bern, 1973), p. 64.

18. Christ's Hospital granted Peele books by Erasmus, Cicero, Terence, Horace, and Ovid in 1571; see Yale ed., 1:30.

19. The poems are reprinted in Yale ed., 1:43–45. On Gager and drama at Christ Church, see C. F. Tucker Brooke, "The Life and Times of William Gager (1555–1622)," *Proceedings of the American Philosophical Society* 95 (1951):403–31.

20. See Yale ed., 1:42; F. S. Boas, *University Drama in the Tudor Age* (Oxford, 1914), Chapters 8 and 9; R. E. Alton, ed., "The Academic Drama in Oxford," *Malone Society Collections* 5 (1960 for 1959):esp. 38–39.

21. Alton, "Academic Drama," p. 65.

22. For the Queen's visits to Cambridge in 1564 and Oxford in 1566, see Boas, *University Drama,* Chapter 5; Elizabeth stayed at Christ Church in 1566.

23. *Friar Bacon and Friar Bungay,* ed. Daniel Seltzer (Lincoln: University of Nebraska Press, 1963), sc. vii, lines 9ff.

24. Yale ed., 1:60–61, quoting Holinshed's description; Boas, *University Drama,* discusses the Alasco visit on pp. 179–81.

25. See below, Chapter 3, for the play's dating (ca. 1581–82).

26. James Peele also wrote pageants; see Jean Robertson and D. J. Gordon, eds., "A Calendar of Dramatic Records in the Books of the Livery Companies of London, 1485–1640," *Malone Society Collections* 3 (1954):45, 46, 50, and 72.

27. S. Schoenbaum, *Internal Evidence and Elizabethan Dramatic Authorship* (Evanston, Ill.: Northwestern University Press, 1966), pp. xvii–xviii, lists the many anonymous plays attributed to Peele. For his possible share in *Titus Andronicus,* see J. C. Maxwell's new Arden edition (1953; rev., London: Methuen, 1961), pp. xxiv–xxvii.

28. Yale ed., 1:55; for comparative purposes, see Edmund K. Chambers's discussion of how much an author earned from writing a play *(The Elizabethan Stage,* 4 vols. [Oxford, 1923] 2:160–64).

29. *Epicoene* (1609), ed. Edward B. Partridge (New Haven: Yale University Press, 1971), 2.3.100–102; as Partridge notes (p. 183) Sir John has managed to confuse the usual distinction between poet and versifier.

Chapter Two

1. For the general argument and many illustrative details, see, respectively: E. W. Talbert, *The Problem of Order* (Chapel Hill: University of North Carolina Press, 1962); Stephen Orgel, *The Illusion of Power: Political Theater in the English Renaissance* (Berkeley and Los Angeles: University of California Press, 1975); Marie Axton, "The Tudor Mask and Elizabethan Court Drama" in Marie Axton and Raymond Williams, eds., *English Drama: Forms and Development* (Cambridge: Cambridge University Press, 1977), pp. 24–47.

2. See Hunter, *John Lyly,* and Daniel Javitch, *Poetry and Courtliness in Renaissance England* (Princeton: Princeton University Press, 1978).

3. A famous example is Elizabeth's response to an entertainment allegorically urging her marriage: "This is all aimed at me" (see Martin Hume, ed., *Calendar of Letters and State Papers . . . preserved in . . . Simancas, 1558–1567* [London: H. M. Stationery Office, 1892], pp. 404–5). Marie Axton analyzes many politically oriented entertainments, especially those at the Inns of Court, in *The Queen's Two Bodies: Drama and the Elizabethan Succession* (London, 1977).

4. Roy Strong, *The Cult of Elizabeth: Elizabethan Portraiture and Pageantry* (London, 1977), p. 129; see Chapter 4. For the celebration's origin, see John Neale, *Essays in Elizabethan History* (New York, 1958), pp. 45–58.

5. M. C. Bradbrook, *The Rise of the Common Player* (London: Chatto and Windus, 1962), p. 251, commenting on the Kenilworth entertain-

ment (1575), but the argument could be extended to connect that entertainment with the one at Woodstock (1592) and Ben Jonson's *Mask of Owls* (1624). See also Axton, "The Tudor Mask," p. 25, and, for tilts, Strong, *The Cult of Elizabeth,* pp. 139–40.

6. The quoted phrase comes from Strong, *The Cult of Elizabeth,* p. 149; see also Bradbrook, *Rise of the Common Player,* p. 247; J. H. Hanford and S. R. Watson, "Personal Allegory in the *Arcadia:* Philisides and Lelius," *Modern Philology* 32 (1934):1–10; Frances Yates, *Astraea: The Imperial Theme in the Sixteenth Century* (London, 1975), pp. 29–111.

7. Gerrarde intends to compliment Elizabeth (green and white were Tudor colors), and his choice recalls a tournament-challenge claiming green and white were not the best colors in Thomas Blenerhasset's *A Revelation of the True Minerva* (1582), a poem filled with allusions to Elizabethan court festivals.

8. The influence may sometimes have gone from tilt-devices into emblem books; see Strong, *The Cult of Elizabeth,* pp. 144–45.

9. Strong believes a portrait of Essex as he appeared at the 1590 Tilt survives (see *Cult of Elizabeth,* illus. 39); more persuasively, Strong argues that Essex's show attempted to palliate Elizabeth's anger at his recent marriage (ibid., p. 152).

10. Peele's nearly contemporary poem *An Eglogue Gratulatorie* (1589) welcomes Essex home from that year's abortive Portuguese expedition. Peele describes him in adulatory pastoral terms as "a great Herdgroome . . . but no swaine, / Save hers that is the Flowre of Phaebes plaine" (48–49). The dialogue devotes three stanzas to the fact that Essex was "Fellow in Armes . . . With that great Shepherd good Philisides" (i.e., Sidney) and finds that in Essex "all his [Sidney's] Vertues sweet reviven bee" (61–62, 74).

11. These lines were originally printed in italics to indicate semiquotation. The phrase "Good Woodman" probably refers to Lee's status as Lieutenant of the Manor of Woodstock, a royal appointment which included the titles "Ranger of the Park and Master of the Game"; see Edmund K. Chambers, *Sir Henry Lee: An Elizabethan Portrait* (Oxford: Clarendon Press, 1936), p. 81. Lee's mention of "his Oraysons" is part of a pattern begun in his 1575 entertainment for Elizabeth and continued in the entertainment of 1592, where he is explicitly called an "owlde Knight, nowe a newe religious Hermite." See A. W. Pollard, ed., *The Queen's Majesty's Entertainment at Woodstock in 1575* (Oxford: n.p., 1903, 1910) and Chambers, *Sir Henry Lee,* pp. 276–97.

12. The manuscript is British Library Additional MS. 21432 (see Frontispiece). Some sections are now illegible; for these portions, the only source is W. S. Fitch's unreliable transcript (printed in Ipswich, ca. 1831). The Yale edition brackets lines deriving from Fitch's transcript, but I have

omitted the brackets. The Yale edition also silently expands abbreviations and does not note Peele's own corrections and changes; I have silently corrected a few errors in the edition.

13. Hastings "leaped for joy," we are told, when Father Henry Walpole broke under interrogation and led his captors to some cached documents; see Mary A. E. Green, ed., *Calendar of State Papers, Domestic Series . . . 1591–1594* (London: H. M. Stationery Office, 1867), p. 417. Since Peele's dedication does not mention Hastings, it probably postdates his death; the countess was a member of the Sidney family, perhaps another reason for Peele's admiration.

14. For a general survey of these episodes, see Martin Hume, *Treason and Plot: Struggles for Catholic Supremacy in the Last Years of Queen Elizabeth* (London: Nisbet, 1901), Chapters 4 and 5.

15. See Arthur Collins, comp., *Letters and Memorials of State,* 2 vols. (London: Osborne, 1746), 1:350.

16. For Wentworth's troubles and the debate over the Act of 1593, see John E. Neale, *Elizabeth I and Her Parliaments 1584–1601* (London: Cape, 1957), pp. 251–66 and 180–97.

17. The coronation entry of 1559 bluntly acknowledges the queen's personal involvement in England's spiritual health; in one pageant she seems indeed to be Time's daughter, Truth. That coronation followed the terrible Marian persecutions, and Peele may be worried, here and elsewhere, that the country now faces similar troubles. See John Nichols, *The Progresses and Public Processions of Queen Elizabeth,* 2d ed., 3 vols. (London: Nichols and Son, 1823), 1:38–60, and Sydney Anglo, *Spectacle, Pageantry, and Early Tudor Policy* (Oxford: Clarendon Press, 1969), pp. 257–58.

18. The pun turns on *écu* and *écusson* ("coat of arms"), cognate with "escutcheon"; cf. *Faerie Queene,* IV:x, and William Higford, *Institution of a Gentleman* (London: W. Lee, 1660), pp. 69–70, which describes this James Skidmore's appearances in the Tiltyard. For the tilts' "neo-medievalism," see Yates, *Astraea,* pp. 108–10, and Strong, *The Cult of Elizabeth,* pp. 161–62.

19. See Rowland Whyte's letter of 22 November 1595 in Collins, *Letters and Memorials,* 1:362; for Bacon's contribution, see James Spedding, Robert Ellis, and Douglas Heath, eds., *The Works of Francis Bacon,* 14 vols. (London: Longman, Green, 1857–74), 8:374–86, and Strong, *The Cult of Elizabeth,* p. 209.

20. For the general outlines of this episode, see John E. Neale, *Queen Elizabeth I* (1934; rev., London: Cape, 1967), pp. 334–36.

21. Some of the printed texts seemed to have been intended as souvenirs of and/or guides to the pageants. Many basic documents and facts are collected in Robertson and Gordon, "A Calendar of Dramatic Records." Peele also wrote a pageant in 1588 (now lost) and probably wrote the

1595 pageant; he may have written those for 1581, 1584, 1586, and 1587; see pp. xxxiv and 56. A standard modern discussion of the shows is David M. Bergeron, *English Civic Pageantry 1558–1642* (London, 1971).

22. Glynne Wickham makes this point about later civic pageants in *Early English Stages, 1300–1660,* vol. 2, part 1 (London: Routledge, Kegan Paul, 1963), p. 237.

23. The word "pageant" signifies both the portable or fixed scaffolding on which various characters sat and from which they delivered their speeches and the entire exhibition itself; "device" refers to the characters and speeches. Thus the title of the Dixi-pageant precisely identifies Peele's contribution as "The Device of the Pageant." See Yale ed., 1:157, and Robertson and Gordon, "A Calendar of Dramatic Records," p. xxii n3.

24. The pageants fascinated foreign visitors. Samuel Kiechel wrote a description of Peele's 1585 effort; he thought the lynx was a camel. See Jean Robertson, ed., "A Calendar of Dramatic Records of the London Clothworkers' Company," *Malone Society Collections* 5 (1960 for 1959):6 n2, and K. D. Haszler, ed., *Die Reisen des Samuel Kiechel,* Bibliothek des litterarischen Vereins in Stuttgart, 86 (1867):26–27.

25. For an account of contemporary Astraea mythology, see Yates, *Astraea,* pp. 29–87.

26. Although the sentiment is a commonplace, it may recall—as does the fountain Superstition and Ignorance wish to poison—Elizabeth's 1559 coronation entry. See above, note 17.

27. Strong, *The Cult of Elizabeth,* p. 173; for the Elizabethan revival, see pp. 165 and 172.

28. Yale ed., 1:96. Since the payment predates the ceremony by three days, Peele may have relied on earlier installations for his description, which lacks any specific details from 1593.

29. The complaint is common; both George Chapman in several early poems and Marlowe himself in *Hero and Leander* (also published in 1593) make similar remarks. D. H. Horne makes the important point that "All five living poets and two of the three contemporary dead ones [mentioned in the prologue] were court writers inclining toward the classical . . ." (Yale ed., 1:96).

30. D. H. Horne comments, in Yale ed., 1:280, "a curious mistake for Salisbury (William Montacute, the second Earl)," but I believe the substitution is deliberate.

Chapter Three

1. See Frank Percy Wilson, *Marlowe and the Early Shakespeare* (Oxford: Clarendon Press, 1953), p. 10, and M. C. Bradbrook, *The Growth and Structure of Elizabethan Comedy,* new ed. (New York: Humanities Press, 1973), p. 46. For the play's date, see Yale ed., 3:8–12.

2. See Yale ed., 1:149–53; a revision appeared in 1604.

3. For the Spenser borrowings, see W. W. Greg, *Pastoral Poetry and Pastoral Drama* (London, 1906), p. 219 and Yale ed., 1:150 and 164.

4. See Greg, *Pastoral Poetry,* p. 223. Andrew von Hendy summarizes negative comment in "The Triumph of Chastity: Form and Meaning in *The Arraignment of Paris*," *Renaissance Drama,* n.s. 1 (1968):87 nl. Von Hendy analyzes many of the literary traditions Peele exploited, especially the medieval ones. In *John Lyly,* G. K. Hunter finds that "the ostensible subject of the play—the judgment of Paris—does not provide a real backbone for a developing dramatic action, and Peele fills out his play with episodes . . . which are only 'scenes from the Classical idylls' " (p. 154).

5. Yale ed., 3:24–50, discusses the play's "Dramatic Tradition"; Hunter's *John Lyly,* Chapter 3, offers an excellent survey of the various literary and dramatic influences on the court dramatist; see esp. pp. 114–35.

6. The Kenilworth entertainment is reprinted in John Nichols, *The Progresses and Public Processions of Queen Elizabeth,* 1:485–523; for *The Lady of May,* see William A. Ringler, Jr., ed., *The Poems of Sir Philip Sidney* (Oxford: Clarendon Press, 1962), and Robert Kimbrough and Philip Murphy, "The Helmingham Hall Manuscript of Sidney's *The Lady of May:* A Commentary and Transcription," *Renaissance Drama,* n.s. 1 (1968):103–19; the Elvetham entertainment is reprinted in R. W. Bond, ed., *The Complete Works of John Lyly,* 3 vols. (Oxford: Clarendon Press, 1902), 1:431–52.

7. Von Hendy, "The Triumph of Chastity," remarks that *The Araygnement*'s opening procession "resembles a summer pageant greeting the Queen on the grounds of an estate" (p. 90).

8. Harold M. Dowling first pointed out this double explanation in "Miscellaneous Notes on Peele," *Notes and Queries* 165 (1933):272–74.

9. See Louis Adrian Montrose, "Gifts and Reasons: The Contexts of Peele's *Araygnement of Paris,*" *ELH* 47 (1980):433–61, for an excellent analysis of this subject and a discussion of the Elizabethan values and contemporary difficulties it reflects.

10. See Yale ed., notes to lines 285 and 579–80, and George Gascoigne, *Complete Works,* ed. J. W. Cunliffe, 2 vols. (Cambridge: Cambridge University Press, 1907–10), 2:125 (the Kenilworth entertainment).

11. The Judgment of Paris is a common subject in Renaissance emblem books; Geoffrey Whitney borrows his illustration (1586) from Joannes Sambucus, *Emblemata* (1564). For further examples, see Arthur Henkel and Albrecht Schöne, *Emblemata: Handbuch zur Sinnbildkunst der XVI. und XVII. Jahrhunderts* (Stuttgart: Metzler, 1967). A similar dramatized ver-

sion (with Elizabeth again the eventual winner) appears in the Elvetham entertainment (1591); see Bond, *Works of Lyly,* 1:431–52.

12. In Robert Greene's *Friar Bacon and Friar Bungay* (ca. 1591), royal visitors to Oxford are entertained with, among other things, a golden tree very like the one Juno shows Paris. Thomas Dekker's *Old Fortunatus* (1599) has many links with *The Araygnement,* including yet another golden tree and a concluding compliment to Queen Elizabeth, before whom the play was presented.

13. C. R. Baskervill's translation, substantially, quoted in Yale ed., 3:124n.

14. The quarto's text often resembles printed descriptions of court masques: the stage directions, especially for the more spectacular effects, are heavily descriptive and in the past tense, and there are "editorial" comments such as "The grace of this song is in the Shepherds Ecco to her verse." The quarto records an occasion as well as a dramatic event or text.

15. This last line reappears as line 41 of *Descensus Astraeae.* Gascoigne and Peele appear to be the only poets who use "Zabeta" as a pastoral name for Elizabeth; see Gascoigne, *Complete Works,* 2:107–17.

16. Peele's resolution—giving Elizabeth the apple—has many analogues in sixteenth-century literature. See John D. Reeves, "The Judgment of Paris as a Device of Tudor Flattery," *Notes and Queries* 199 (1954):7–11, with additional possibilities in Inga-Stina Ekeblad [Ewbank], "On the Background of Peele's 'Araygnement of Paris,' " *Notes and Queries,* n.s. 3 (1956):246–49, and Elkin Calhoun Wilson, *England's Eliza* (Cambridge, Mass., 1939), pp. 147–48.

17. See Leslie Hotson, ed., *Queen Elizabeth's Entertainment at Mitcham: Poet, Painter, and Musician* (New Haven: Yale University Press, 1953), pp. 11–12.

18. For texts of the last two, see respectively, Bond, *Works of Lyly,* 1:417–19, and Alexander B. Grosart, ed., *The Works in Verse and Prose . . . of Sir John Davies,* 3 vols. (London: Blackburn, 1869–76), 1:272–89, and see Strong, *The Cult of Elizabeth,* p. 52.

19. Allan Holaday, gen. ed., *The Plays of George Chapman: The Comedies* (Urbana: University of Illinois Press, 1970), p. 569.

20. For *The Lady of May,* see Kimbrough and Murphy, "The Helmingham Hall Manuscript," p. 106. Ernest W. Talbert has examined the idea that praise and flattery and teaching of the courtly audience went hand-in-hand; see "The Interpretation of Jonson's Courtly Spectacles," *PMLA* 61 (1946):454–73, where he discusses many forms of entertainment including masques, royal entries, and country house revels.

21. In "The Structural Significance of Myth and Flattery in Peele's *The Arraignment of Paris,*" *Studies in Philology* 65 (1968):163–70, Henry G. Lesnick argues that Elizabeth is, implicitly, a "Christ-like redeemer of

Trojan progeny" (p. 169). Thus, the Trojan and Christian myths justify the "flattery" at the play's conclusion.

22. Bradbrook, *Growth and Structure of Elizabethan Comedy,* pp. 242 n8 and 98; cf. the long section on "Envy" in *Anglorum Feriae,* lines 114–52, and see Charles Read Baskervill, *English Elements in Jonson's Early Comedy* (Austin: University of Texas Press, 1911), pp. 158–62 and 286–89.

23. For "liberation," see Bergeron, *English Civic Pageantry 1558–1642,* pp. 57 and 63.

24. See Axton, "The Tudor Mask," pp. 27ff.

25. For a modern edition, see Bond, *Works of Lyly,* 1:471–90.

Chapter Four

1. Yale ed., 3:319–41, examines the sources closely.

2. The play does not specify that the three are "pages," but their names, attitudes, and actions make the assumption likely.

3. See Yale ed., 3:438, note to line 639.

4. See S. Musgrove, "Peele's 'Old Wives Tale': An Afterpiece?" *AUMLA* 23 (1965):94. I have elaborated Musgrove's argument a little.

5. These are the principal (and some picayune) objections the Yale editor lists and partly discusses on 3:339–43. Most of the complaints may be found in Harold Jenkins, "Peele's 'Old Wive's Tale,' " *Modern Language Review* 34 (1939):177–85, and in John Crow, "Folklore in Elizabethan Drama," *Folk-Lore* 58 (1947):297–311.

6. The phrase "neither maid, nor widow, nor wife" appears in *Measure for Measure* (see Yale ed., 3:426–27, note to line 183). *The Oxford Dictionary of English Proverbs,* 3d ed., rev. F. P. Wilson (Oxford: Clarendon Press, 1970), cites the proverb in 1578; it could imply that the woman was a whore.

7. A general principle of enchantment seems to be that victims require external help to escape; they cannot unenchant themselves. A wholly logical approach to magic is useless: Venelia is Sacrapant's victim, but nonetheless manages to extinguish the magic light once he is dead.

8. The Yale editor plausibly believes that Peele has blended two folklore stories, each of which had its own means of killing the sorcerer (Yale ed., 3:331–32). The beheading and use of a prop head also make theatrical sense because they visually demonstrate the young/old transformations of Erestus and Sacrapant.

9. See Gordon H. Gerould, *The Grateful Dead* (London, 1907).

10. These last two examples are mentioned, with others, in Yale ed., 3:346–47; Frank Hook wisely comments, "One might almost say that redundancy is the rule of the play" (3:347).

11. F. B. Gummere, ed., *The Old Wives Tale,* in *Representative English Comedies,* comp. Charles M. Gayley, 4 vols. (New York, 1903–36) 1:341.

12. See Gwenan Jones, "The Intention of Peele's 'Old Wives' Tale,' " *Aberystwyth Studies* 7 (1925):93 and 79, respectively.

13. For example, see Gummere, *The Old Wives Tale,* 1:344; Cheffaud, *George Peele* (Paris, 1913), p. 116; Yale ed., 3:341.

14. Frank Hook shows that the play's supposedly realistic dialogue has rhetorical structure (Yale ed., 3:361–64), but even this demonstration is superfluous, since it shows us—what we already knew—that "realism" in drama is conventional and requires as much artistry as any nominally "unrealistic" art.

15. Laurilyn J. Rockey, in "*The Old Wives Tale* as Dramatic Satire," *Educational Theater Journal* 22 (1970):268–75, tries to show such connections but fails. Gwenan Jones, "The Intention of Peele's 'Old Wives' Tale,' " claims that Peele's plot is not a parody because it is less exaggerated than the plays it supposedly mocks (p. 87). The best recent treatment of these earlier plays is Patricia Russell, "Romantic Narrative Plays: 1570–1590," in *Elizabethan Theatre,* ed. J. R. Brown and Bernard Harris (London, 1966); she shows that they themselves contain elements of self-parody (pp. 121, 124, and 127).

16. See Musgrove, "Peele's 'Old Wives Tale': An Afterpiece?"

17. Cheffaud, *George Peele,* pp. 121–28, identifies Huanebango as Gabriel Harvey; the arguments are rejected in Yale ed., 3:311–19.

18. Crow, "Folklore in Elizabethan Drama," p. 305.

19. Thelma Greenfield, in *The Induction in Elizabethan Drama* (Eugene, Oreg., 1969), says it is "unique in its delicate blending of the frame and the play" (p. 106) and "*The Old Wives Tale* and *The Knight of the Burning Pestle* are the finest examples of the artistic integration of induction and play" (p. 155).

20. See for example, Hunter, *John Lyly,* pp. 154 and 247, and Muriel C. Bradbrook, "Peele's *Old Wives' Tale:* A Play of Enchantment," *English Studies* 43 (1962):323.

21. Basic information concerning the company may be found in Chambers, *Elizabethan Stage,* 2:104–15, and in Alexander Leggatt, "The Companies and the Actors" in Clifford Leech and T. W. Craik, gen. eds., *The Revels History of Drama in English, Volume III, 1576–1613* (London: Methuen, 1975); for their court performances, see p. 50.

22. See Chambers, *Elizabethan Stage,* 2:114 and note, and R. A. Foakes and R. T. Rickert, eds., *Henslowe's Diary* (Cambridge, 1961), p. 7.

23. The most cautious range of dates for its composition would be after 1588 (because of the anti-Spanish remarks at lines 364, 385, and 388) and before 8 May 1594 (when the Queen's Men disbanded) or at the latest 16 April 1595 (when the play was entered in the *Stationers' Register*). For a full discussion, see Yale ed., 3:306–11.

24. Jenkins, in "Peele's 'Old Wive's Tale,' " argues for a cut text; his views are refuted by Musgrove, "Peele's 'Old Wives Tale': An Afterpiece?" and see Yale ed., 3:341–56.

25. Chambers, *Elizabethan Stage,* 3:48, thinks the staging resembles court staging. See also Yale ed., 3:373–76, Senn, *Dramatic Construction,* p. 3, and Susan T. Viguers, "The Hearth and the Cell: Art in *The Old Wives Tale,*" *Studies in English Literature* 21 (1981):209–21.

26. See Yale ed., 3:355; *Edward I,* another public theater play, has an extremely large cast (see ibid., 2:46 and 70–71). Although adult actors could sing, the fact that Anticke, Fantasticke, and Frolicke do so in consort makes it likely they were played by boys.

27. The Yale editor concludes: "the play could be performed equally well on the public stage or at court" (3:376).

28. See Yale ed., 3:359, and Rockey, "*The Old Wives Tale* as Dramatic Satire," p. 275, respectively.

29. See Thomas L. Berger and William C. Bradford, Jr., comps., *An Index of Characters in English Printed Drama to the Restoration* (Engelwood, Colo.: Microcard Editions Books, 1975), and for *Endymion,* see Bond, *Works of Lyly,* 3:5–80. "Venelia" and "Erestus" are also known only in *The Old Wives Tale,* although "Erastus" appears in two approximately contemporary plays and "Eristus" in Lyly's *Midas.*

30. John Doebler believes that the connection verges on parody; see "The Tone of George Peele's *The Old Wives' Tale,*" *English Studies* 53 (1972):412–21, esp. pp. 414, 417, and 419.

31. Bond, *Works of Lyly,* 3:20.

Chapter Five

1. John Yoklavich discusses Peele's treatment of his sources in Yale ed., 2:236–47.

2. This statement assumes that the play was first performed before 1591 and revived about 1598–1601; for further details, see below and Yale ed., 2:221–26, and W. W. Greg, *Two Elizabethan Stage Abridgements* (Oxford, 1923), pp. 7–16 and 85–93.

3. Yoklavich argues that *The Explanation* provided the anti-Spanish material for the play (Yale ed., 2:278). In fact, Polemon's *The Second . . . booke of Battailes* may have directed Peele to *The Explanation.* After his account of the Battle of Alcazar, Polemon describes how Don Antonio resisted the Spanish invasion; in "The Battaile of Lisbon" (Polemon, sigs. Y3r–Y4v) marginal references to *The Explanation* appear. Even if Peele found *The Explanation* independently, these references prove the pamphlet's currency in 1587.

4. For the historical background, see R. B. Wernham, "Queen Elizabeth and the Portugal Expedition of 1589," *English Historical Review* 66

(1951):1–26 and 194–218; *The Battle of Alcazar* "predicts" the Armada at lines 686–88.

5. The best biography of Stukeley, and my source, appears in Richard Simpson, ed., *The School of Shakspere,* 2 vols. (London: Chatto and Windus, 1878), 1:158–268; John Izon's *Sir Thomas Stucley c. 1525–1578 Traitor Extraordinary,* The Rogue's Gallery, no. 4 (London: Melrose, 1956), is romanticized but contains some good illustrations and a treatment of the European political context.

6. Quoted from Thomas Fuller's *Worthies of England* in Yale ed., 2:247n.

7. Simpson, *School of Shakspere,* 1:144–51, reprints the surviving ballad material and Yale ed., 2:266–70, collects some other references. For "stewtly," see Judith C. Levinson, ed., *The Famous History of Captain Thomas Stukeley,* Malone Society Reprints (Oxford: Malone Society, 1975 for 1970), p. viii.

8. Alleyn played the Moor's part in the revival of *The Battle of Alcazar* (see Greg, *Abridgements,* pp. 70 and 92), and there is no reason to doubt he did so in the original production.

9. Alexander Dyce, in *The Works of George Peele,* 2d rev. ed. (London, 1829–39) 2:96n, quotes Tamburlaine's final line: "For Tamburlaine, the scourge of God, must die." Cheffaud, *George Peele,* pp. 75–77 and 82, gives many convincing examples of Peele's "spirit of emulation."

10. The main discussions of all three problems are Greg, *Abridgements,* pp. 7–8, 15–16, and 94–101, and Yale ed., 2:218–26 and 286–87. My own account depends on these two.

11. Greg, *Abridgements,* p. 21; Greg reproduces and analyzes the "plot" of this play.

12. Ibid., pp. 85–93, where Greg argues for April 1598 to February 1599; arguments that the revival took place in late 1600 or after are summarized in Foakes and Rickert, *Henslowe's Diary,* pp. 329–31.

13. The Admiral's Men were apparently out of London between 1591 and mid-1594; see Greg, *Abridgements,* pp. 17–20.

14. Greg, *Abridgements,* p. 101, and see Yale ed., 2:287–88.

15. The plot does not contain any information about Act 5, which has, moreover, suffered heavily from cutting and revision.

16. Polemon praises Abdelmelec as "a verie proper man. . . . He was ingenious, sharpe witted, and passing prudent and wise" (sig. Y2v); Peele diverges from the source in making Muly Mahamet Seth into an equally admirable character (cf. Polemon, sig. Y2r).

17. Cf. Yale ed., 2:243, where Yoklavich finds *Alcazar*'s coherence superior to that of Marlowe's *Edward II,* a view I doubt.

18. See Senn, *Dramatic Construction,* p. 91: "causation is implicit, in a general way, in the finality of the story, and the story itself was no doubt well known to the audience."

19. Although Yoklavich does not think so: see Yale ed., 2:241.

20. Senn, *Dramatic Construction,* p. 93, remarks how Peele has made the meeting ironic.

21. As Greg says, "the text of this scene has been very considerably cut and altered, many episodes being reduced to mere scuffle and noise" (*Abridgements,* p. 118).

22. Senn, *Dramatic Construction,* p. 94, but his own analysis often ignores the point.

23. See Dieter Mehl, *The Elizabethan Dumb Show* (London, 1965), p. 80.

24. See Clarence W. Mendell, *Our Seneca* (New Haven: Yale University Press, 1941), pp. 197–98, on the way Elizabethan dramatists used Seneca's rhetorical horrors.

25. Yoklavich says "he is practicably to be identified with some eyewitness of the battle" (Yale ed., 2:348).

26. Lines 21 and 22 have puzzled editors, but a paraphrase might be: Let the audience sit and be silent like these dramatic characters who were silenced through being murdered ("of murther" means "by murder") by their brother ("by kind" means "by a relative"). Cf. "This Moore, this murtherer of his progenie" (980).

27. The same suitably Senecan proverb appears in *Gorboduc* (1562) and *Horestes* (1567).

28. Cheffaud, *George Peele,* pp. 81–83; see also Mehl, *The Elizabethan Dumb Show,* p. 82. Senn, *Dramatic Construction,* pp. 57–58, reviews the critical debate over the sources of the play's structure.

29. *A Warning for Fair Women,* Induction, lines 43–50, in Simpson, *The School of Shakspere,* 2:242–43.

30. See Nicholas Brooke, "Marlowe as Provocative Agent in Shakespeare's Early Plays," *Shakespeare Survey* 14 (1961):35–36, and Bernard Spivack, *Shakespeare and the Allegory of Evil* (New York: Columbia University Press, 1958), pp. 379–86.

31. Cheffaud, *George Peele,* p. 78, argues forcefully for the Moor's crime as the source of the play's plot and action. Senn, *Dramatic Construction,* pp. 58–59, seems to agree, but later sees "a theme (revenge)" as "the shaping factor" (p. 126), although he also mentions Sebastian's "honor" or "ambition" as a further source of "shape and coherence" (p. 90).

32. Elizabethan discussion of the queen's successor often returned to the house of Lancaster; see R. Doleman, *A Conference about the Next Succession* ("N.," 1594), Part 2, Chapter 4, and below, Chapter 6 and note 20.

Doleman considers the Portuguese claim to the English throne and Don Antonio's special case in Part 2, Chapter 8.

33. Eldred Jones, *Othello's Countrymen: The African in English Renaissance Drama* (London, 1965), p. 43; Aaron *(Titus Andronicus)* and Eleazer *(Lust's Dominion)* are Jones's other main examples. He goes on to argue that Peele also provides the soon-to-be-standard contrast between the black or "Negro Moor" and the light-skinned "'white' Moor" (here, Abdelmelec); see p. 49.

34. Ibid., p. 45.

35. As Jones does, I think; see ibid., pp. 47–48.

36. Senn, *Dramatic Construction,* pp. 127–29, attacks the play's power of characterization and downplays the theatrical value of the Abdelmelec-Moor contrast (see, e.g., pp. 151–52).

37. Jones, *Othello's Countrymen,* p. 48.

38. See, e.g., Yale ed., 2:243, and Senn, *Dramatic Construction.*

39. For contemporary Elizabethan political conditions and their reflection in the drama, see Emrys Jones, *The Origins of Shakespeare* (Oxford: Clarendon Press, 1977), Chapter 5.

40. See Senn, *Dramatic Construction,* pp. 127–28.

Chapter Six

1. See *King Edward the First,* ed. W. W. Greg (Oxford: Malone Society, 1911), pp. v–vi, and Yale ed., 2:1 and 9. The 1599 quarto reprints that of 1593.

2. See Foakes and Rickert, *Henslowe's Diary,* pp. 317 and 323.

3. Yale ed., 2:39–40, minimizes the problem of performing the 1593 text, although a mediocre script could be made without great effort. A modern attempt to do just that appears as a "retroform": see G. K. Dreher, ed., *The Chronicle of King Edward the First* (Chicago, 1974).

4. See Chambers, *Elizabethan Stage,* 2:148–49, and Yale ed., 2:8, for financial calculations.

5. See above, Chapter 4. Alfred Hart, *Stolne and Surreptitious Copies* (Melbourne, 1942), pp. 375–76, gives a succinct account of theatrical affairs 1587–94. On the united acting companies, see Greg, *Two Elizabethan Stage Abridgements,* pp. 17–20, and Chambers, *Elizabethan Stage,* 2:120–24; for Pembroke's Men, their plays, and possible connections with both *The Battle of Alcazar* and *Edward I,* see Hart, *Stolne and Surreptitious Copies,* pp. 352–90.

6. *Longshanks* first appears in Henslowe's accounts almost two years after *Edward I*'s first printing with the marginal notation "ne." On the possible meanings for this term, see Yale ed., 2:8–9, and Foakes and Rickert, *Henslowe's Diary,* pp. xxx–xxxi and 30.

7. In "The Text of Peele's *Edward I*," Dora Jean Ashe argues for revision by "anon."; Frank Hook argues for Peele. Both believe that the Queen Elinor material has been either added or expanded from its original length. Senn, *Dramatic Construction,* pp. 131–34, usefully undermines this latter view. Cheffaud, *George Peele,* pp. 93–94, believes that Peele added the Robin Hood episodes to his original play.

8. See Leo Kirschbaum, "A Census of Bad Quartos," *Review of English Studies* 14 (1938):36. Yale ed., 2:37–39, answers the argument effectively.

9. Senn, *Dramatic Construction,* pp. 62 and 153; the Yale editor's views are hard to make out: see Yale ed., 2:15–17 and 47–48.

10. See Senn, *Dramatic Construction,* pp. 95–97.

11. For consistency's sake, I adopt the spellings of the Yale editor's *dramatis personae* (2:70–71).

12. See Irving Ribner, *The English History Play* (London, 1965), pp. 89–90.

13. Peele may have drawn the "potter" from an extant ballad; see Yale ed., 2:18, and R. B. Dobson and J. Taylor, comps., *Rymes of Robyn Hood: An Introduction to the English Outlaw* (London: Heinemann, 1976), pp. 43–44, 123–32, and 215–19.

14. Lines 2653–68 are misplaced, and lines 2661–66 virtually repeat lines 2011ff.

15. For further details of Peele's historical sources and their treatment, see Yale ed., 2:10–16, and Cheffaud, *George Peele,* p. 96. Senn, *Dramatic Construction,* p. 62, summarizes: "He [Peele] thus attempted to replace the episodic, chronological method by a more dramatic one, in which the material is arranged in terms of the central problem, Edward's fight for supremacy threatened by insurrection."

16. Irving Ribner, *The English History Play,* p. 85.

17. Shakespearean examples include *King John, Richard II,* and the two parts of *Henry IV.* The chronological relation of *Edward I* and *Edward II* is much debated; the plays have four passages in common and *Edward II* also borrows from *The Battle of Alcazar;* see H. B. Charlton and R. D. Waller, eds., *Edward II,* rev. ed., F. N. Lees (London: Methuen, 1955), pp. 8–10 and 173, respectively.

18. For the negative view, see Ribner, *The English History Play,* p. 89, and, less critically, Cheffaud, *George Peele,* pp. 93–94.

19. For the appropriate passages from *The Mery Geste,* see Dobson and Taylor, *Rymes of Robyn Hood,* pp. 104–11. The poem existed in manuscript from about 1500. Disguising appears in nearly every Robin Hood tale and in Munday's play. Anne Barton's "The King Disguised: Shakespeare's *Henry V* and the Comical History," in Joseph G. Price, ed., *The Triple Bond* (University Park: Pennsylvania State University Press, 1975), pp. 92–117, examines the many disguised-king plays of the 1590s.

20. *A Conference* probably postdates all three plays, but the crisis and the Spanish claim had been common subjects for decades; Doleman's book and the various replies to it may help explain *Edward I*'s popularity during the mid-1590s. See above, Chapters 2 and 5. Materials on the genesis and impact of *A Conference* appear in L. Hicks, S.J., "Father Robert Persons, S.J. and *The Book of Succession*," *Recusant History* 4 (1957–58):104–37.

21. Marie Axton, *The Queen's Two Bodies,* p. 101. Axton's entire discussion (Chapter 7) of the history plays in the 1590s repays study, although she fails to show that Edmund is more important, technically, to the Spanish claim than Queen Elinor is: see Doleman, *A Conference,* Part 2, Chapter 2.

22. *Descensus Astraeae* was written before 29 October 1591 (when it was performed) and probably printed shortly thereafter. The quoted line also appears in Marlowe's *Edward II;* see the edition cited in note 20, above, 3.2.33 and p. 220.

23. See Yale ed., 2:199, note to stage direction after line 2361.

24. Ibid., note to lines 704ff., where some important puns are explained.

25. For "ore prie," the palm trees, and fountains as eyes, see ibid., 2:183, note to line 723.

26. The Yale editor thinks so (2:29–30), but the analogous heading in *The Araygnement of Paris* after line 852 weakens his case. Two formal orations in Shakespeare's *Richard III,* 5.3, also have their own headings.

27. Ashe, "The Text of Peele's *Edward I*," discusses some of the stage directions on pp. 157–60, and *Soliman and Perseda* (ca. 1590) has some similar directions.

28. Horace, *Epistles,* 1.2.69, quoted from *Satires, Epistles and Ars Poetica,* trans. H. R. Fairclough, Loeb Library (London: Heinemann, 1926).

29. See Yale ed., 2:22, for the tale's typical form.

Chapter Seven

1. See L. B. Campbell, *Divine Poetry and Drama in Sixteenth-Century England* (Berkeley and Los Angeles, 1959), Part 2, Chapter 9, "Biblical Plays in the Public Theatres." She notes that while "Bible plays were continuously being offered at the public theatres . . . only two which can with some confidence be assigned to the public theatres have been preserved" (p. 246). In fact, the theatrical auspices of *David and Bethsabe* are unknown; there is no contemporary production record. See Yale ed., 3:143, and Foakes and Rickert, eds., *Henslowe's Diary,* p. 217.

2. See the introduction to 1 and 2 Samuel in *The New Oxford Annotated Bible,* expanded ed. (New York: Oxford University Press, 1977), p. 330.

3. For consistency's sake, I have retained Peele's preferred spelling of biblical proper nouns, although they often differ from the conventional modern ones.

4. In *The Endeavors of Art* (Madison: University of Wisconsin Press, 1954), p. 102, Madeleine Doran remarks, "Peele's *David and Bethsabe* and *Edward I* . . . are good examples of shapeless unselectivity of incident." Wolfgang Clemen, however, shows that "To do justice to Peele's plays, we must not judge them according to the normally accepted standards of dramatic unity and structure; they must be judged by criteria that are appropriate to their special character" (Wolfgang Clemen, *English Tragedy Before Shakespeare: The Development of Dramatic Speech,* trans. T. S. Dorsch [London, 1961], p. 163).

5. The Geneva translators' introduction to the Second Book of Samuel says simply, "In the persone of David the Scripture setteth forth Christ Jesus the chief King, who came of David according to the flesh." When quoting or citing the Bible, I have used the facsimile of the 1560 Geneva translation, edited by Lloyd E. Berry (Madison: University of Wisconsin Press, 1969), modernizing the orthography slightly.

6. Senn, *Dramatic Construction,* pp. 64–69, tabulates Peele's rearrangements of his biblical subject matter. Cheffaud, *George Peele,* pp. 129–30, 137–41, and 176–85, has shown that Peele also borrowed heavily from the work of the French religious poet Du Bartas.

7. While this description of the play's organizing idea is not incompatible with Inga-Stina Ewbank's influential and acute interpretation, they are not quite the same. In "The House of David in Renaissance Drama," *Renaissance Drama* 8 (1965):3–40, Ewbank examines *David and Bethsabe*'s literary context and finds that "Peele's guiding idea" is "the effects of David's sin on his House" (p. 19), that "David's guilt . . . is the thematic unifier" (p. 30), and that "Peele is primarily after . . . the working out of moral and civil disorder within the House of David" (p. 36). See also Yale ed., 1:93, and Senn, *Dramatic Construction,* p. 102.

8. The text, never very good, is extremely corrupt at this point. The choric speech is labeled "5. Chorus" and mentions a "third discourse of Davids life" (1581); a random piece of text (a stage direction, three lines of a speech by Absalon, and a catchword) follows immediately. For further details and speculation on what has happened, see Yale ed., 3:178–79 and 188, and Bruno Neitzel, *George Peele's "David and Bethsabe"* (Halle: H. John, 1904), pp. 51–54.

9. Ewbank also finds this passage "*Lycidas*-like" ("The House of David," p. 39), as does Campbell, *Divine Poetry and Drama,* p. 259.

Chapter Eight

1. Ronald B. McKerrow, ed., *The Works of Thomas Nashe,* rev. ed., F. P. Wilson, 5 vols. (Oxford: Blackwell, 1958), 3:323.

2. Alexander B. Grosart, ed., *The Life and Complete Works in Prose and Verse of Robert Greene,* 15 vols. (reprint ed., New York: Russell and Russell, 1964), 12:141–43.

3. For other literary associates, see Yale ed., 1:65–70.

4. Larry M. Robbins, *Thomas Dekker's A Knights Conjuring (1607): A Critical Edition* (The Hague: Mouton, 1974), pp. 155–56.

5. See above, Chapter 5, and Yale ed., 1:78.

6. David Horne analyzes the age-old quality of the stories in *The Merrie Conceited Jests;* see Yale ed., 1:110–26.

7. Frank Percy Wilson, *Marlowe and the Early Shakespeare* (Oxford: Clarendon Press, 1953), p. 10.

8. For example: Edward Tandy, ed., *The Poetry of George Peele* (Christ's Hospital, London, 1927); *Twice So Fair* (Leicester, England, 1970); Sally Purcell, ed., *George Peele* (South Hinksey, England, 1972).

9. W. W. Greg, *The Old Wives Tale New Vampt* (London: Sidgwick and Jackson, 1911) and W. H. Auden and Chester Kallman, "Delia," *Botteghe Oscure* 12 (1953):164–210.

10. See above, Chapter 7, note 4.

11. Hunter, *John Lyly,* pp. 154 and 247; see also Senn, *Dramatic Construction,* pp. 205–6.

12. Bradbrook, "Peele's *Old Wives' Tale:* A Play of Enchantment," p. 324.

13. Senn, *Dramatic Construction,* and Inga-Stina Ewbank, " 'What words, what looks, what wonders?': Language and Spectacle in the Theatre of George Peele" in *Elizabethan Theatre V* (Toronto, 1974), pp. 124–54.

14. Hunter, *John Lyly,* p. 349.

15. John Polemon, *The Second . . . booke of Battailes* (London, 1587): "the gard tooke the king from his horse, and layd him in his horselitter, where he gave upp the Ghost within halfe an houre after. Yet his death was subtilly dissembled, they bruting that he was layd downe to rest him" (sig. X3r).

16. The first phrase is Greene's (see above, note 2) and the second is from Nashe's Preface to *Menaphon* in *Works,* 3:312.

17. Hunter, *John Lyly,* p. 297, remarks "the curious gap in the literary life of the time . . . 'The University Wits' expired quickly as a generation, leaving no obvious progeny."

Selected Bibliography

Sixteenth-century titles have been slightly modernized; the primary bibliography lists only important modern editions or ones often omitted from printed bibliographies. In annotations, Peele's canonical plays have been abbreviated as follows: *Alcazar* (for *The Battle of Alcazar*); *Araygnement* (for *The Araygnement of Paris*); *David* (for *David and Bethsabe*); *Edward* (for *The Chronicle of King Edward the First*); *OWT* (for *The Old Wives Tale*).

PRIMARY SOURCES

1. Printed and Manuscript

Anglorum Feriae. British Library Additional MS. 21432.

Anglorum Feriae: Englandes Hollydayes. Transcribed by W. Stevenson Fitch. Ipswich, England: Privately Printed, ca. 1831.

The Araygnement of Paris: A Pastorall. London, 1584.

The Battell of Alcazar. London, 1594.

The Chronicle of King Edward the First. Edited by G. K. Dreher. Chicago: Adams Press, 1974. A rearranged text.

Descensus Astraeae. London, 1591.

The Device of the Pageant borne before Woolstone Dixi. London, 1585.

An Eglogue Gratulatorie. London, 1589.

The Famous Chronicle of King Edward the First. London, 1593.

The Famous Chronicle of King Edward the First. London, 1599.

A Farewell Entituled to the Famous and Fortunate Generalls . . . Sir John Norris and Sir Frauncis Drake [with] *A Tale of Troy.* London, 1589.

The Honour of the Garter. London, 1593.

The Hunting of Cupid. [Excerpts in] *Englands Helicon.* London, 1600; *Englands Parnassus.* London, 1600.

The Hunting of Cupid. [Excerpts in] Drummond MS. 7, folios 352–53 and 361 [in Library of Society of Antiquaries, Edinburgh].

The Love of King David and Fair Bethsabe. London, 1599.

The Old Wives Tale. London, 1595.

The Old Wives Tale. Edited by F. B. Gummere. In: *Representative English Comedies.* Compiled by Charles M. Gayley. 4 vols. New York: Macmillan, 1903–36. Volume 1.

The Old Wives Tale. London: Sidgwick and Jackson, 1911. A version by Walter W. Greg.

The Old Wives Tale. Edited by Patricia Binnie. The Revels Plays. Manchester, England: Manchester University Press, 1980.

Polyhymnia. London, 1590.

The Praise of Chastity. [In] R. S., *The Phoenix Nest.* London, 1593.

The Tale of Troy. London, 1604.

2. Collected and Selected Works

George Peele. Compiled by Sally Purcell. South Hinksey, England: Carcanet Press, Fyfield Books, 1972. Selections.

The Life and Works of George Peele. Charles Tyler Prouty, general editor. 3 vols. New Haven: Yale University Press, 1952–70.

The Poetry of George Peele: A Selection. Compiled by Edward Tandy. Christ's Hospital, London: The Outlook, 1927.

Samples from David and Bethsabe. Compiled by G. K. Dreher. Chicago: Adams Press, 1980. With passages from Coverdale's translation of the Bible and commentary.

Twice So Fair. Leicester, England: Offcut Press, 1970. Selections.

The Works of George Peele. Edited by Alexander Dyce. 2d rev. ed., 3 vols. London: William Pickering, 1829–39.

The Works of George Peele. Edited by Arthur H. Bullen. 2 vols. London: John C. Nimmo, 1888.

SECONDARY SOURCES

1. Bibliographies

Daves, Charles W. "George Peele." In: *The Predecessors of Shakespeare: A Survey and Bibliography of Recent Studies in English Renaissance Drama.* Edited by Terence P. Logan and Denzell S. Smith, pp. 143–52. Lincoln: University of Nebraska Press, 1973. Items generally restricted to 1923–1968 with many omissions; some helpful annotation.

Johnson, Robert C. *Elizabethan Bibliographies Supplements* 5, pp. 59–63. London: Nether Press, 1968. Incomplete secondary bibliography, 1939–1965.

Ribner, Irving, and **Huffman, Clifford C.** *Tudor and Stuart Drama.* 2d ed. Goldentree Bibliographies in Language and Literature, pp. 95–97. Arlington Heights, Illinois: AHM, 1978. Selective.

Tannenbaum, Samuel A. *George Peele (A Concise Bibliography).* Elizabethan Bibliographies 15. New York: S. Tannenbaum, 1940. Lists 587 items including early printings, editions, and dissertations.

2. General

Alton, R. E., ed. "The Academic Drama in Oxford: Extracts from the Records of Four Colleges." *Malone Society Collections* 5 (1960 for 1959):29–95.

Ashe, Dora Jean. "The Non-Shakespearean Bad Quartos as Provincial Acting Versions." *Renaissance Papers* (1954), pp. 57–62. *Edward* mentioned (p. 57) as a "bad" quarto.

———. "The Text of Peele's *Edward I.*" *Studies in Bibliography* 7 (1955):153–70. Argues for anonymous revison and finds the play a "good" quarto.

Ashley, Leonard R. N. *Authorship and Evidence: A Study of Attribution and the Renaissance Drama, Illustrated by the Case of Peele 1556–96.* Etudes de philologie et d'histoire 6. Geneva: Droz, 1968. Idiosyncratic study, mentioning Peele occasionally.

———. *George Peele.* New York: Twayne, 1970. Discusses most of the works; attention to literary associations.

Auden, Wystan Hugh, and **Kallman, Chester.** "Delia or A Masque of Night." *Botteghe Oscure* 12 (1953):164–210. Libretto for a one-act opera based on *OWT.*

Axton, Marie. *The Queen's Two Bodies: Drama and the Elizabethan Succession.* Royal Historical Society Studies in History. London: Royal Historical Society, 1977. Important discussion of *Alcazar* and *Edward.*

Ball, B. W. "George Peele's Huanebango: A Caricature of Gabriel Harvey." *Renaissance Papers* (1968), pp. 29–39. Unconvincing.

Bergeron, David M. *English Civic Pageantry 1558–1642.* London: Edward Arnold, 1971. Examines Peele's mayoral pageants.

Boas, Frederick S. *University Drama in the Tudor Age.* Oxford: Clarendon Press, 1914. Comprehensive; some mention of Peele.

Bradbrook, Muriel C. "Peele's *Old Wives' Tale:* A Play of Enchantment." *English Studies* 43 (1962):323–30. *OWT* probably written for a provincial audience.

Brooke, C. F. Tucker. "The Life and Times of William Gager (1555–1622)." *Proceedings of the American Philosophical Society* 95 (1951):401–31. Brief mention of Peele.

Campbell, Lily Bess. *Divine Poetry and Drama in Sixteenth-Century England.* Berkeley and Los Angeles: University of California Press, 1959. Discusses *David* in context of religious drama.

Chambers, Edmund K. *The Elizabethan Stage.* 4 vols. Oxford: Clarendon Press, 1923. Essential reference work.

Cheffaud, P. H. *George Peele (1558–1596?).* Paris: Felix Alcan, 1913. Valuable critical comment; factual material outdated.

Chew, Samuel C. *The Crescent and the Rose: Islam and England during the Renaissance.* New York: Oxford University Press, 1937. Discusses *Alcazar* and King Sebastian (pp. 526–30); brief mention of other works by Peele (pp. 482–86).

Clapp, Sarah Lewis Carol. "Peele's Use of Folk-Lore in *The Old Wives' Tale*." [University of Texas] *Studies in English* 6 (1926):146–56. A general survey.

Clemen, Wolfgang. *English Tragedy Before Shakespeare: The Development of Dramatic Speech.* Translated by T. S. Dorsch. London: Methuen, 1961. Chapter 11 is devoted to Peele's plays.

Cox, John D. "Homely Matter and Multiple Plots in Peele's *Old Wives Tale*." *Texas Studies in Language and Literature* 20 (1978):330–46. Argues for unity of *OWT*'s plots.

Craik, T. W. "The Reconstruction of Stage Action from Early Dramatic Texts." In: *Elizabethan Theatre V.* Edited by George R. Hibbard. Toronto: Macmillan, 1974, pp. 76–91. Examines stage action in *David.*

Crow, John. "Folklore in Elizabethan Drama." *Folk-Lore* 58 (1947):297–311. Almost entirely devoted to *OWT.*

Cutts, John P. "Peele's *Hunting of Cupid.*" *Studies in the Renaissance* 5 (1958):121–32. Suggests that the work was a pastoral poem and prints music for one song.

Dean-Smith, Margaret. "The Ominous Wood: An Investigation into Some Traditionary Sources of Milton's *Comus*." In: *The Witch Figure: Folklore Essays*. Edited by Venetia Newall. London: Routledge, Kegan Paul, 1973, pp. 42–71. Comments on *OWT*.

De Stasio, Clotilde. "Il linguaggio drammatico di George Peele." *English Miscellany* 15 (1964):61–87. Ably shows the dramatic (as opposed to lyric) quality of the plays' language.

Doebler, John. "The Tone of George Peele's *The Old Wives' Tale*." *English Studies* 53 (1972):412–21. *OWT* is a parody of "the fairy-tale chivalric romance."

Doleman, R. [pseud.] *A Conference about the Next Succession to the Crowne of Ingland.* "N." [Antwerp? St. Omer?], 1594 [1595?]. Influential two-part treatise on the subject.

[Ewbank], Inga-Stina Ekeblad. "On the Background of Peele's 'Araygnement of Paris.' " *Notes and Queries,* n.s. 3 (1956):246–49. Lists classical and contemporary antecedents.

Ewbank, Inga-Stina. "The House of David in Renaissance Drama: A Comparative Study." *Renaissance Drama* 8 (1965):3–40. Excellent study of *David* and its dramatic tradition.

———. " 'What words, what looks, what wonders?': Language and Spectacle in the Theatre of George Peele." In: *Elizabethan Theatre V*. Edited by George R. Hibbard. Toronto: Macmillan, 1975, pp. 124–54. Defends the spectacular dramaturgy of Peele's plays.

Foakes, Reginald A., and **Rickert, R. T.,** eds. *Henslowe's Diary.* Cambridge: Cambridge University Press, 1961. Standard modern edition of important source for theatrical history.

Gerould, Gordon H. *The Grateful Dead.* London: Folk-Lore Society, 1907. Discusses folkloric elements in *OWT.*

Goldstone, Herbert. "Interplay in Peele's *The Old Wives' Tale.*" *Boston University Studies in English* 4 (1960):202–13. Discusses relation of plot elements.

Gordon, Cosmo. "The First English Books on Bookkeeping." In: *Studies in the History of Accounting.* Edited by A. C. Littleton and B. S. Yamey. London: Sweet and Maxwell, 1956, pp. 202–5. Mentions James Peele throughout.

Greenfield, Thelma N. *The Induction in Elizabethan Drama.* Eugene: University of Oregon Books, 1969. Discusses *Alcazar* and praises frame structure of *OWT.*

Greg, Walter W. *Pastoral Poetry and Pastoral Drama.* London: Bullen, 1906. Places *Araygnement* in tradition of pastoral writing.

———. *Two Elizabethan Stage Abridgements.* Oxford: Clarendon Press, 1923. Analyzes "plot" of *Alcazar.*

Habicht, Werner. *Studien zur Dramenform vor Shakespeare: Moralität, Interlude, romaneskes Drama.* Anglistische Forschungen 96. Heidelberg: Carl Winter, 1968. Brief mention of *Araygnement;* extended treatment of *OWT.*

Hart, Alfred. *Stolne and Surreptitious Copies: A Comparative Study of Shakespeare's Bad Quartos.* Melbourne: Melbourne University Press, 1942. Passing comments on several plays by Peele.

Howarth, Robert G. *Diary, Drama, and Poetry: Presentations and Recoveries.* Capetown, South Africa: University of Capetown Department of English, 1971. Offers a comprehensive analysis of *OWT* (pp. 165–75).

Hunter, George K. *John Lyly: The Humanist as Courtier.* London: Routledge, 1962. Penetrating discussion of late sixteenth-century English culture; Peele mentioned frequently.

———. *Lyly and Peele.* Writers and Their Work 206. London: Longmans, 1968. Very brief study which finds Lyly a better dramatist than Peele.

Jenkins, Harold. "Peele's 'Old Wive's Tale.' " *Modern Language Review* 34 (1939):177–85. Concludes that the text suggests the play was performed on a provincial tour.

Jones, Eldred. *Othello's Countrymen: The African in English Renaissance Drama.* London: Oxford University Press, 1965. Discusses *Alcazar* (pp. 40–49) and the Dixi pageant (pp. 29, 34–35).

Jones, Gwenan. "The Intention of Peele's 'Old Wives' Tale.' " *Aberystwyth Studies* 7 (1925):79–93. Important essay arguing that play is folkloric and not literary satire.

Koeppel, Emil. *Ben Jonson's Wirklung auf zeitgenössische Dramatiker und andere Studien.* Anglistische Forschungen 20. Heidelberg: Carl Winter, 1906. Lists allusions to and quotations from Peele in contemporary plays (pp. 51–62).

Larsen, Thorleif. "A Bibliography of the Writings of George Peele." *Modern Philology* 32 (1934):143–56. Complete descriptions of early editions of Peele's canonical works.

———. "The Historical and Legendary Background of Peele's 'Battle of Alcazar.' " *Transactions of the Royal Society of Canada* 33, section 2 (1939):185–97. Cites many contemporary and near-contemporary allusions to Stukeley.

Lesnick, Henry G. "The Structural Significance of Myth and Flattery in Peele's *The Arraignment of Paris*." *Studies in Philology* 65 (1968):163–70. Suggests Christian associations for the play's subject matter.

Lucazeau, Michel. "L'*Irene* de Peele retrouvée? Compte rendu d'enquête." *Etudes Anglaises* 31 (1978):340–59. Unconvincingly identifies Peele's suppositious, but unknown, play *The Turkish Mahomet and Hiren the Fair Greek* with Gilbert Swinhoe's *The Unhappy Fair Irene* (1658).

Marx, Joan C. " 'Soft, Who Have We Here?': The Dramatic Technique of *The Old Wives Tale*." *Renaissance Drama* n.s. 12 (1981):117–43. *OWT* contains numerous, unparodied genres, and its structure is "one of generic contrast created by a purposeful technique."

Mehl, Dieter. *The Elizabethan Dumb Show: The History of a Dramatic Convention*. London: Methuen, 1965. Discusses *Araygnement* (pp. 78–80) and *Alcazar* (pp. 80–82).

Miller, Edwin Haviland. *The Professional Writer in Elizabethan England: A Study of Nondramatic Literature*. Cambridge, Mass.: Harvard University Press, 1959. Useful study which mentions Peele briefly.

Montrose, Louis Adrian. "Gifts and Reasons: The Contexts of Peele's *Araygnement of Paris*." *ELH: Journal of English Literary History* 47 (1980):433–61. Studies the cultural implications of gift-giving in the play and in Elizabethan society.

Musgrove, S. "Peele's 'Old Wives Tale': An Afterpiece?" *AUMLA* 23 (1965):86–95. Argues that *OWT* was designed to "follow after a comedy."

Neale, John E. *Essays in Elizabethan History*. New York: St. Martin's Press, 1958. Includes essays on Accession Day (pp. 45–58) and the event it celebrates (pp. 59–84).

Pearn, B. R. "Dumb-Show in Elizabethan Drama." *Review of English Studies* 11 (1935):385–405. Partial listing with comparative comments.

Polemon, John. *The Second part of the booke of Battailes, fought in our age*. London, 1587. Principal source for *Alcazar*.

Reeves, John D. "The Judgment of Paris as a Device of Tudor Flattery." *Notes and Queries* 199 (1954):7–11. Studies the history of this *topos* in sixteenth-century literature of all kinds.

Ribner, Irving. *The English History Play in the Age of Shakespeare.* Rev. ed. London: Methuen, 1965. Discusses *Edward* on pp. 85–91; other mentions of Peele throughout.

Robertson, Jean, and **Gordon, Donald J.,** eds. "A Calendar of Dramatic Records in the Books of the Livery Companies of London, 1485–1640." *Malone Society Collections* 3 (1954). Records of James and George Peele's mayoral pageants.

Robertson, Jean, ed. "A Calendar of Dramatic Records of the London Clothworkers' Company." Addenda to *Malone Society Collections* 3 in *Malone Society Collections* 5 (1960 for 1959):1–16. Additional records.

Rockey, Laurilyn J. "*The Old Wives Tale* as Dramatic Satire." *Educational Theater Journal* 22 (1970):268–75. Unconvincing.

Roston, Murray. *Biblical Drama in England: From the Middle Ages to the Present Day.* Evanston, Ill.: Northwestern University Press, 1968. Discusses *David.*

Russell, Patricia. "Romantic Narrative Plays: 1570–1590." In: *Elizabethan Theatre.* Edited by J. R. Brown and Bernard Harris, pp. 107–29. Stratford-upon-Avon Studies 9. London: Edward Arnold, 1966. Full study of the plays *OWT* may satirize.

Sampley, Arthur M. "Plot Structure in Peele's Plays as a Test of Authorship." *PMLA* 51 (1936):689–701. Considers *Araygnement, David,* and *Edward.*

Saunders, J. W. *The Profession of English Letters.* London: Routledge, Kegan Paul, 1964. Brief and sometimes inaccurate mention of Peele.

Senn, Werner. *Studies in the Dramatic Construction of Robert Greene and George Peele.* Swiss Studies in English 74. Bern: Francke, 1973. Useful, rigidly formalistic study of *Alcazar, David,* and *Edward.*

Sheavyn, Phoebe. *The Literary Profession in the Elizabethan Age.* Manchester, England: Manchester University Press, 1909. Useful on social and economic matters; the 1967 rev. ed. (by J. W. Saunders) is unreliable on Peele.

Stanley, Emily B. "The Use of Classical Mythology by the University Wits." *Renaissance Papers* (1956), pp. 25–33. Defends Peele's use of mythology to organize plays and "enhance mood."

Strong, Roy. *The Cult of Elizabeth: Elizabethan Portraiture and Pageantry.* London: Thames and Hudson, 1977. Chapter 4 analyzes Accession Day tilts, including Peele's.

Viguers, Susan T. "The Hearth and the Cell: Art in *The Old Wives Tale.*" *Studies in English Literature* 21 (1981):209–21. Argues that *OWT* dramatizes the conflict between false art (Sacrapant) and true (Madge); comments on staging.

Von Hendy, Andrew. "The Triumph of Chastity: Form and Meaning in *The Arraignment of Paris*." *Renaissance Drama,* n.s. 1 (1968):87–101. A general study of the play.

Wilson, Elkin Calhoun. *England's Eliza.* Harvard Studies in English 20. Cambridge, Mass.: Harvard University Press, 1939. A comprehensive but largely taxonomic study which mentions most of Peele's civic and courtly poems.

Wilson, Robert H. "Reed and Warton on *The Old Wives Tale.*" *PMLA* 55 (1940):605–8. Demonstrates that Isaac Reed was the first to identify (in 1782) the similarities between *OWT* and Milton's *Comus.*

Yates, Francis A. *Astraea: The Imperial Theme in the Sixteenth Century.* London: Routledge, Kegan Paul, 1975. Mentions Peele in chapters on Elizabeth as Astraea (pp. 29–87) and on Accession Day tilts (pp. 88–111).

Index